Edith Deutsch

HELPING YOUR ALCOHOLIC BEFORE HE OR SHE HITS BOTTOM

HELPING YOUR ALCOHOLIC BEFORE HE OR SHE HITS BOTTOM

A Tested Technique for Leading Alcoholics into Treatment

by Roque Fajardo

CROWN PUBLISHERS, INC., NEW YORK

To my other self,
my wife, Dorothy

Inquiries should be addressed to Crown Publishers, Inc., One Park Avenue, New York, N.Y. 10016.

Published simultaneously in Canada by General Publishing Company Limited

Printed in the United States of America

Designed by Ruth Kolbert Smerechniak

LIBRARY OF CONGRESS CATALOGING IN PUBLICATION DATA

Fajardo, Roque.
Helping your alcoholic before *he or she hits bottom*
1. Alcoholics—Family relationships. 2. Alcoholics —Rehabilitation. 3. Alcoholism. I. Title.
HV5132.F34 1976 362.2'92 76-15380
ISBN 0-517-52682-4

Contents

Acknowledgments

Many people helped make this book. They include my late father, Jose Fajardo; my mother, Rosario Erice Hagan; my grandfather, Dionisio Erice; Dr. Armando Jimenez of San Jose de las Lajas, Cuba; my son, Chris; his grandfather, Emmett Wilcox.

The late Tennessee Governor Frank G. Clement; John W., Jack K., George G., and Joe M. of AA; Judge Henry F. Todd; Salvation Army Major Wilbur Young; Mary C. Stephens; Reverend Dennis Mary McAuliffe. O.P.; the late Mgsr. Thomas P. Duffy; Leonard Morgan, Ph.D.; Leo Robert Ryan, Ph.D.; Joseph Fishbein, M.D.

Ed Shea; G. J. Tarleton, M.D.; Thomas P. Wall, L.L.D.; Kenneth Schoen; James M. Gallagher, Jr.; Clara Hieronymus; T. Cecil Wray; Owsley R. Cheek; William Ridley Wills, II; Bernard Werthan, Jr.; Victor Coode; F. C. ("Doc") Wallace and Willard F. ("Bill") Bailey—Samaritans all.

Frank W. Stevens, M.D.; George Mann, M.D., St. Mary's Hospital, Minneapolis, Minnesota; Anderson Spickard, M.D., Vanderbilt University Hospital; Genevra Ziegler-Driscoll, M.D., Eagleville Hospital and Rehabilitation Center, Eagleville, Pennsylvania.

Mark B. Sobell, Ph.D., Vanderbilt University; Linda C. Sobell, Ph.D., Dede Wallace Alcohol Programs, Nashville, Tennessee; John Siegenthaler; Jordan Stokes, III; Morris Adkins; Ray Silva; Julian Gant, M.C.; Bishop Joseph A. Durick; the late Msgr. A. A. Siener; my colleagues Kittie Myatt, Karen Czaplicki, Anne Bowman, and Patti Pyle.

Special thanks are due Ben C. Liebermann, A.C.S.W., former director, division on alcoholism, Tennessee Department of Mental Health; Lloyd Elam, M.D., president, Meharry Medical College; the late Eric Bell, Jr., M.D.; the late Charles Moss; Orrie A. Couch, Jr., M.D.; Brainard Cheney, and Reverend Joseph L. Kellermann, executive director, Charlotte, North Carolina, Council on Alcoholism. Finally, to David McDowell and Herbert Michelman of Crown Publishers.

Foreword

Helping Your Alcoholic Before *He or She Hits Bottom* explodes the myth that an alcoholic cannot be helped unless he wants help. It spells out *where* and *when* and *how* a husband or wife of an alcoholic can take positive steps and learn to cope with his or her own problems and bring about basic changes in an alcoholic marriage.

The book is not written in professional jargon but in clear simple language that spells out what steps a family can take if they are willing to go through the painful process of changing themselves. It is not a magic answer but a description of guided intervention—not by making the alcoholic do what we want him to do or stop doing what we do not want him to do.

It tells us how we can change our reaction and response to the alcoholic. The purpose is motivating the alcoholic to enter a recovery program, not just to stop drinking.

Alcoholism is never an illness of one person. It is always a matter of excessive drinking, which results in disruptive consequences, the reaction of others to the drinker and a response that results in another drinking cycle. The way in which family, friends, and others react to the alcoholic perpetuates the illness or opens the door to recovery.

Helping Your Alcoholic Before *He or She Hits Bottom* is a message of hope for any family member who wishes to help an alcoholic recover. It deals with the all-important matter of responsibility. It is painful to watch an alcoholic destroy himself and his family. It is even more painful initially to learn how to confront the alcoholic, face reality, and intervene in behalf of the family and the alcoholic.

The family system conditions family members to react to alcoholism in ways that are predictable, normal, protective, and destructive. Without judging the family or the alcoholic, Roque Fajardo discusses the process of alcoholism and the roles that are being played. Instead of focusing on the alcoholic and all the skills that might be used in counseling the alcoholic, he reverses the process and discusses frankly what is happening to the family. Reading his book is like hearing a coach explain to his team how they lost the game and describe the hard, painful practice sessions that must be performed repeatedly if the team is to overcome their mistakes and learn how to win games instead of losing.

This important new book is a refreshing, stimulating experience for it is written out of years of experience of working in the field of alcoholism with family, friends, and employers, not just alcoholics. It abandons the medical model that simply does not fit alcoholism and deals with the areas of responsibility of the next of kin and others. It may shock some professionals who have become immune to the fact that the vast majority of alcoholics never enter any program of recovery. It goes right to the heart of the matter—that the way family members react to alcoholics helps destroy the family, including the alcoholic, or by a learned process can result in guided intervention and recovery.

Helping Your Alcoholic Before *He or She Hits Bottom* is a manual for anyone who loves an alcoholic and wants to learn how to help the alcoholic recover.

Joseph L. Kellermann,
Executive Director,
Charlotte Council on Alcoholism, Inc.,
Charlotte, North Carolina

We know that some land in jail, some in the asylum, and that some commit suicide. . . . It is very rare indeed that an alcoholic addict comes to a psychiatrist voluntarily. It is usually by reason of medical, legal, or moral—sometimes physical—compulsion from without. . . . The reason for this does not lie in some wicked perverseness but in the deep hopelessness and despair from which every alcoholic secretly suffers. For him the efforts of any person or institution to relieve him of his alcohol habit is as if they would rob him of the only relief he has from unendurable suffering.

—*KARL MENNINGER,* Man Against Himself, *1938*

Moreover if thy brother shall trespass against thee, go and tell him his fault between thee and him alone: if he shall hear thee, thou hast gained thy brother. But if he will not hear thee, then take with thee one or two more, that in the mouth of two or three witnesses every word may be established. And if he shall neglect to hear them, tell it unto the church: but if he neglect to hear the church, let him be unto thee as an heathen man and a publican.

—MATTHEW 18:15—18. 1st century A.D.

1

Guided Intervention Can Save an Alcoholic Marriage

There is an epidemic of alcoholism in the United States today that is still not seriously challenged. The latest figures place the number of victims at between nine and thirty million. One of many reasons the epidemic goes unchallenged is that the word *epidemic* itself usually is applied to the excessive prevalence of a disease, and there is no agreement in the scientific world about the phenomenon known as alcoholism, "drinking problem," chemical dependency, or alcohol addiction. Is it a disease? The United States Supreme Court determined a few years ago that the disease label was still open to scientific question. Perhaps it matters a great deal to classify it properly, but while researchers and antisearchers debate the question, the fact remains that millions of useful and worthy Americans are dying from it and millions more are being wasted, sacrificed, and damaged in tragic ways.

The ambivalence of our national attitudes toward alcoholism, plus the occasional reports of research challenging the idea that alcoholics can never safely drink again, feeds the tragic pattern of the pathological delusions of the alcoholic and helps millions to postpone any attempt to get help and treatment.

Even as you read this, several million seemingly successful Americans are desperately pouring their first drink of the day. With trembling hands they gulp the lifesaving liquid without which they could not make it to the office. Or they might be going through doors marked "Hospital Personnel Only." Some are teachers who will tell impressionable students about Sinclair Lewis or Hemingway's ability to become literary giants in spite of alcohol. Others are successful mothers and wives helping their last child go off to school. Smiling, exchanging small talk with their husbands, they keep to themselves their crying, desperate need for their first of many drinks of the day.

THE CONCERNED PERSON

It is not yet quite a cliché to say that an alcoholic is not a skid row bum because so many still do not comprehend it. But it is an important truth. Probably 90 percent or more of all alcoholics are economically and socially above skid row. As the founder and director of a treatment agency, the Samaritan Center, I have worked with indigent alcoholics for over twelve years, and I am still uncertain as to the definition of skid row. But probably 60 to 70 percent of all alcoholics are gainfully employed or are homemakers holding up their end of the economic and social responsibilities of the marriage contract. It is important that we consider these figures because it means we are often working alongside or living with an alcoholic long before we ever suspect it.

This is written to benefit those millions of Americans who

must get help and be rescued from their alcoholic shackles, because what happens finally is up to them—but what starts the recovery may not be. I do not expect to reach them first. This message is directed to the concerned person living closest to these tragic human beings. The concerned person suffers frustration and perplexity and sometimes is driven to near insanity, desperation, or even to alcohol.

In speaking of the concerned person I shall use the female gender because today wives appear to outnumber husbands in this category. But none of us should forget the primary victim, the alcoholic. He is my intended beneficiary, and I do not want a spouse or other person to abandon him. That can be a death warrant.

In all that has been written and spoken about alcoholism in our time, no greater mischief has been created than that done by spreading the idea that it is impossible to help an alcoholic who refuses help, or who refuses to admit he is an alcoholic or has a drinking problem. If this were true, very few of the millions who have found sobriety and a degree of serenity and success would have succeeded. The truth is that probably more than half of all alcoholics who overcome the tragedy have done so at the instigation, suggestion, and coercion of some concerned person. About half the treatment process of alcoholism involves getting the victim to admit he has a problem and to accept help. Whenever the alcoholic really knows and accepts the truth of his addiction—at "gut level," as we say in group therapy—about half the treatment has been accomplished. The process of accepting the diagnosis is probably the most difficult part of achieving recovery from alcoholism. For years I have known many alcoholics who have not accepted themselves as true addicts of alcohol even after repeated tragedy, near death, and traumatic economic and social experiences.

I have seen many persons attend meetings of Alcoholics Anonymous (where custom virtually requires the member to begin every talk with the words *I am an alcoholic*) who have repeated the public words of confession over and over and have also remained sober over several years but have not really internalized its meaning. When we take the attitude that the alcoholic must admit he has a problem before he can be helped, we are excluding virtually all of them. We are excluding the millions and millions of sensitive, intelligent, creative, useful leaders and other contributors to the general welfare who are alcoholics and who are committing mass suicide in slow motion while we wait for them to "hit bottom" and admit their problem.

Most alcoholics do not accept help or admit their problem until they do hit *a* "bottom." But one man's bottom is another man's mezzanine. A friend of mine in AA likes to explain his own case. "Most alcoholics don't wake up until they hit the bottom or the basement," he says, "but I got off at the mezzanine floor and I'm grateful to AA for that."

What is not so generally acknowledged by recovering alcoholics is that somebody outside themselves created their bottom or, more accurately stated, created the turning point in their lives that prompted them to accept some kind of help.

The turning point can vary widely in the lives of many alcoholics and we sometimes tend to attribute too much importance to it, particularly if we are alcoholics ourselves who think we are passed it. Sometimes a turning point cannot be identified until years later. Some of the more memorable turning points told to me by recovering alcoholics are simple. For a divorced woman alcoholic it occurred when after attending AA meetings for eighteen months without abstaining from alcohol, members of her family told her unequivocally that unless she did something about her problem they would go to court and take her children away from her. She immediately became responsive to what she had been hearing at the AA meetings.

A favorite turning point story of mine is one about the wife who finally gave up her battle to keep her husband from drinking. When he came down to breakfast one morning, in place of bacon and eggs there was a bottle of whiskey at his place. The real punch line to this story is what he said when he saw the bottle of booze: "What are you trying to do, kill me?" Before that he claimed that his wife was trying to kill him by denying him alcohol. Now he recognized the truth at gut level for the first time. It was the whiskey that would kill him unless somebody helped him. And so he got serious about AA.

In another case the husband was the concerned person. Giving up on his alcoholic wife's drinking after having tried many things, he gathered up their children and their necessities and moved out. In the middle of the living-room floor he left a full case of whiskey. "If you want to drink yourself to death, here it is. The children and I are gone." And his wife started accepting help.

In these three examples the alcoholics responded by internalizing, that is, by recognizing in their deepest levels of conscious understanding that they were about to lose the most important people in their lives. First, the divorced mother was about to lose her children; then a man, his wife; and finally, a mother was going to lose both husband and children.

It might seem that fear of death might be effective as an event to turn alcoholics toward sobriety. But it isn't. An alcoholic is rarely frightened into recovery. I knew a former insurance company executive who had become an indigent alcoholic and who told this story. He would display a red tag he carried in his shirt pocket. The tag bore a notation with his name and stated that he had been found virtually dead from drinking rubbing alcohol. The red tag had been attached to his meager belongings after he had been taken to a hospital. But he had lived to tell the story. "I'll always carry this [he would say, flashing the tag] to remind me that I can't drink." But only a few months later he did begin drinking again and he was found dead shortly thereafter.

GUIDED INTERVENTION

In my opinion it is not that alcoholics are less afraid of death than the average person but that they delude themselves into believing that they are not going to die while drinking and that they are going to live forever when they aren't drinking. What really does work for turning them away from almost certain death or insanity? The answer lies in giving them a dependable, attainable, tangible alternative. It must be dependable. It must be attainable. It must be tangible, and it must be presented as an alternative. I call this technique Guided Intervention.

Almost every spouse of an alcoholic to whom I have told this in the past has invariably told me it wasn't true. "I've tried what you say. It didn't work." Then they cited an example of what they did that failed: "I told him a dozen times I'd leave him if he didn't quit. And once I actually did move out of the house." I cannot say how many times I have heard that protest. But this was not a dependable alternative. The spouse always came back or backed down too soon. There was no guided intervention but misguided game playing. The threats and promises proved to be empty and grew even less effective with time and repetition.

One woman told me her husband said he would drink twice as much if she insisted on going to meetings of Al-Anon, the fellowship for wives and husbands of alcoholics. She stopped going because she knew beyond any doubt that her husband would increase his drinking as he promised. When she threatened to move out he knew she would not do it. "I've got four teen-age children to take care of," this beleaguered wife told me. "Who would support us if he decided to leave?" Her alcoholic husband's words obviously were dependable and very tangible, and he continues to drink and she continues to live in bondage and fear.

THE CO-ALCOHOLIC

There are literally millions of wives today who are afraid to act lest their alcoholic mates increase their drinking, leave them, or refuse to support them. What can be done to help these prisoners of alcoholism? Aren't they truly just as much in the clutches of demon rum as their mates? They are. I call them co-alcoholics, for a person who shares the attitudinal problems of an alcoholic is the closest thing to being an addict.

The answer to this problem is becoming evident to more and more alcoholism counselors all over the United States. Those who are not the direct victims of alcohol still have a chance of seeing the light, taking advice, and leading marriage partners or loved ones to sobriety and safety. I woke up to these facts after I worked with several hundred indigent alcoholics who had lost their families, friends, and employers. I discovered that something might have been done for them much earlier when I saw allegedly hopeless case after hopeless case respond to treatment and slowly find his way back to respectability and sobriety. I discovered the effectiveness of my residential treatment center in helping alcoholics—and yet how weak it was in comparison to that of almost any wife.

It dawned on me then that millions of wives might do something while they still had their alcoholic husbands at home. Yes, here at Samaritan Center, my center, were the alcoholic husbands who had bullied and driven their wives to distraction while they drank themselves into unemployment and disaster and finally familylessness. Here at Samaritan Center were these bullies of another time, another place, now tamed and helpless and almost hopeless finding their way back. I discovered that when I was able to get their wives or former wives back into the picture and if this wife would take my counseling, we succeeded practically every time. It was only when the wife gave up that we failed. The question then naturally arose: If wives were so important, and if they could make the difference between successful recovery and failure, why did it have to wait so long? Why did it happen five, ten, and even fifteen years after the home had broken up, children left fatherless for years—their most important years—to be raised by a mother who had to be a breadwinner, too? Why?

The answer was that they didn't have to wait, that wives could help their alcoholic husbands to find lasting sobriety if they only knew what to do and what not to do. The continuing tragedy of Samaritan Center wives was that most of them would not believe their former husbands had really quit or that they could. Many times Samaritan men had been sober six months, a year, and even longer, and yet their former wives—those who were contacted and had not remarried—refused to believe the truth even when they were handed tangible proof.

A recurring experience I had with many of the men was to agree to intercede with ex-wives after a long and significant period of sobriety by their husbands. These were wives who had not known their husbands to stay sober as long as a week in their last few years together and who had known their husbands had been in a skid row existence. So when a stranger called them on the telephone or came to see them in person and told them of their former husband's long period of sobriety, of the changes he was undergoing, more often than not they would slam the receiver down or close the door or refuse to talk. Fear—unreasonable, irrational, blinding fear of one more disappointment—made them refuse to reconsider or even talk about their former mates. Theirs was the terrible fright of a person who has been hurt too many times, and too deeply, by the same bitter experiences of a husband who promised but failed to stay sober.

"I've made a whole new life for myself and the boys," the first such wife whose help I sought told me when I called her. She had not seen her former spouse for some five years at the time. In heartbreak and despair she had finally divorced him after he had been discovered by police committing a minor burglary to get money to drink. She had divorced him while he served a jail term. "I cannot and I won't go through again what I've been through once," she told me. "I like my life now and I love my boys, and I can't let him come back and ruin all our lives again."

Another one was much less articulate. I talked to her in a beauty shop where she was surrounded by clean, attractive women, all bent on looking even more attractive, clean, and prosperous, and enjoying the good things of life. I remember how struck I was by the difference in her beauty salon and the kind of places her husband—a onetime very successful salesman—had been frequenting before coming to our center. She was curt and cold. She practically denied her former husband's very existence. "As far as my children and I are concerned, he's dead," she told me. And after only a few minutes she had me convinced. I was not the one who could bring back to life the man she had for all purposes buried and forgotten, although he was very much alive, in the same city, and frequently less than a block away from her. But geographic distance means nothing where memory and feelings, mind and fear, are concerned. And so I had to admit defeat. I told him not to give up, that perhaps when she heard it from me, his ex-wife and the mother of his children just might reconsider. He assured me I would be wasting my time, that his former wife would not reconsider taking him back even as an acquaintance or as an ex-husband and the father of her children. So when I returned he tried to hide his tiny ray of hope but immediately accepted the grim truth that I had to give him.

Please note that I was not trying to reunite people in second marriages. I knew what many counselors know. Sometimes it is much better for the alcoholic and the spouse that they not remarry. Sometimes sobriety shows a spouse that when the alcoholic stopped drinking and stayed sober their marriage could not survive. This is no social theory. It is a plain and simple truth. But it is not true in the majority of cases.

It needs to be said that no person can create an alcoholic. Alcoholics tilt their own drinks. No one can know when to offer the alcohol in the right quantities and at the precise times that will cause another to become an alcoholic because no one knows how much it would take or how individuals differ. Every drinker largely determines his own drinking pattern. There are also psychological considerations that play a part, and there is other evidence that heredity may play a part. Although these factors are not scientifically certain yet, there is enough evidence to take them into account. The part one human being may play in the shaping of an alcoholic is just as difficult to ascertain. No one can be blamed with certainty for causing alcoholism in another person, and no one should have guilt feelings about it.

LIFESAVING TECHNIQUE

But with guided intervention there are many things a person can do to help an alcoholic respond, and finally—if he himself elects to—find recovery. That is a different proposition. Suppose that you are swimming with someone who starts to swim across a stream and suddenly confesses to you that he cannot go on. You might become a lifesaver even if you never had the Red Cross lifesaving course. But if you are like many persons concerned with alcoholics (or co-alcoholics), you may drown your companion while trying to save him. Many years ago when I took a lifesaving course, I was told to knock out the failing swimmer if he would not accept my efforts to save his life. In trying to help an alcoholic it is sometimes necessary to use a figurative blow on the head with a two-by-four to accomplish the job.*

Let me continue this analogy of guided intervention to rescue alcoholics with lifesaving techniques. Suppose the drowning person continues to insist that he is *not* drowning and that he actually enjoys gulping down the water he is swimming in. Suppose he insists even after going down the second time that everything is all right. Suppose he keeps screaming, "Don't touch me! Can't you see I'm all right? I'm going to be okay!" And all the while we see that he is just about to go down for the last time. Would we be justified in not trying to force our rescue on him? There isn't time for this kind of consideration. Obviously, Red Cross instructors who taught giving a blow to the head were ready to impose their wills on another person to save that person's life.

I happen to believe in every person's right to choose his own destiny and life-style. But if he chooses to live with me or share my life in other ways, then he becomes involved in

*A remarkable paper, "Therapy with a Two-by-Four: Challenge to the Therapist" by Rea Killoy Stoll, University of Kansas, *Journal of Social Welfare,* Winter 1974, makes this point for professionals.

"To a great extent, until recently, the helping professions have given up on the chemical abuser. And understandably so, for any one given group of people can be pulled through the loophole of manipulations just so many times before it becomes totally exhausted and transfers its energy output to more productive projects. However, it is the easy way out to decide that the chemical abuser cannot be helped. It is much more difficult to think that we might have to change our therapeutic approach. A change in therapeutic approach which breaks through the manipulative ploy of the chemical abuser, in my opinion, is of utmost importance if we want to talk about any sort of effective treatment and rehabilitation. In essence, we must learn to *not trust* him. Not only our professional training has made this task difficult for us but our Judeo-Christian cultural heritage has made us uncomfortable about not trusting people. . . ."

my philosophy and my preferences, and I may have to give him a chance to make a choice that may involve losing my company or sharing my house. If this person is my spouse and I discover that she is slowly killing herself because of alcohol addiction, then I believe I must help her in every possible way to conquer that addiction, even if it involves losing me. If I love someone enough to marry her it means that if possible we should share everything in our lives together. But if I discover that she is committing suicide in slow motion by excessive drinking, I could not continue to share my life with her. It is impossible. No one can.

It is impossible to share a life with a practicing alcoholic. No one can share a life with any person who is so unpredictable as to be a paragon of decorum one day and be urinating on the floor the next. It is impossible to share a life with an alcoholic who simply drinks himself into a stupor each night in front of the television set or shuts himself off in another place in the house or who does his drinking away from home. To believe this is sharing a life is to delude oneself. That is precisely what millions of co-alcoholics (or persons concerned with alcoholics) are doing every day of the year.

If one is living with an alcoholic in a marriage worth saving, one has some choices. But first let's consider what is an alcoholic marriage "worth saving" in the sense that the nonalcoholic spouse should assume responsibility. I believe an alcoholic marriage is worth saving if the alcoholic loves you and you love him. If you don't really love him or if he doesn't truly love you, then he himself may be worth saving but not the bankrupt marriage. The absence of love would be an impediment to sobriety. The chances are very good that you couldn't succeed in saving the "marriage" or the alcoholic even if you tried. The trouble here is that alcoholism must take precedence over marital failure, because marital failure cannot be repaired while alcoholism is an active problem.

ALCOHOLICS AND INFIDELITY

It is true that love often dies in alcoholic marriages, but not always and not necessarily permanently. This is something for the co-alcoholic to decide. Sometimes the death of love goes unnoticed in the hullabaloo of other things. And sometimes alcoholic marriages get temporary staying power by the entrance of a lover for the co-alcoholic. The cases where the alcoholic mate takes a lover are much rarer in my experience and so rare as not to merit attention at this point. I have never found a spouse of an alcoholic who was putting up with the twin problem of alcoholism and infidelity. The reason seems to be that ethyl alcohol satisfies more and is more enticing than a mere human.

But whenever a co-alcoholic spouse approaches me about how to reach her alcoholic mate, I quickly determine whether there is true love in the marriage or if the nonalcoholic mate has found some relief with a lover. If the co-alcoholic wife does have a boyfriend, I tell her that we probably won't succeed because love is a prerequisite in guided intervention, and if there is a third party, love is diminished and is not strong enough to weather the pressures that achieving success will entail.

Sometimes the co-alcoholic admits that she has a lover or boyfriend (or that she has had one but is in the process of terminating the relationship) and insists on trying anyway. The prognosis for success is guarded because another deterrent to success in guided intervention for conquering alcoholism is the existence of harmful delusions. When a woman is able to ask for professional help for an alcoholic husband who has already been pushed aside for another man, a second powerful delusion hangs heavy over the marriage.

Three such cases come to my mind in my experience. One was a professional man, living in an expensive suburban home. He told me how he had been horrified to discover that the nightly shared "drink before dinner" with his wife was not really her first, but frequently her sixth or seventh. But later he had agreed to ration her a "fifth" every other day. He accepted her reasoning that as long as that amount did not increase it would be safe.

A "fifth" is a fifth of a gallon, 25.6 fluid ounces of liquor, meaning he allowed her almost 13 ounces a day. She weighed about 100 pounds. This meant that her 13 ounces a day was the equivalent of 20 ounces a day for the hypothetical average American of 150 pounds.

I told him at the time that he had in effect agreed to help

her kill herself. He said he had decided that for himself. But he confessed that he had another woman in another city whom he had been seeing and would continue to see because she was his true love. It was no surprise then when several weeks later after only about two visits and several canceled appointments he told me by phone that he had a discussion with his wife and had once again agreed with her that as long as it didn't increase, the "fifth" ration every other day was not out of line and would help her get through her menopause, one of her several excuses for drinking herself into oblivion every day.

Then there was the woman co-alcoholic seeing me about her alcoholic husband. After many visits she broke down and confessed to having had an affair with her minister. Over a period of time I urged her to make a choice between her husband and the clergyman-lover, and she insisted in not seeing a connection between the problem of her husband's drinking and her very secret affair while her husband continued his drinking.

None of the three co-alcoholics I have mentioned loved their alcoholic spouses enough to make the sacrifices necessary to help them to recovery, although all three deluded themselves into believing they did. The alcoholic marriage worth saving is one in which the alcoholic loves and is loved in return by the spouse or whose love and whose spouse's love is not permanently extinguished. Many times helping the alcoholic to recover makes love blossom anew and is the start of a second honeymoon.

Some argue that a spouse no more than anyone else has a right to interfere with the freedom of choice of the alcoholic person to continue his life of harmful drinking even though it is going to bring about early death, bad health, bad relationships, and so on. It is a personal decision much as the one that parents must make about spanking children. But when a two- or three-year-old child manages to slip out and cross a dangerous street more than once, a spanking delivered at the time gets across the message that must be conveyed. Often a child has a hard time understanding the danger of death or serious injury in mere words. A spanking conveys the message at a "feeling" level!

In my opinion, if a person married to an alcoholic decides

that she does not have a "right to interfere," then what she is really saying is that she does not love her husband enough to interfere. If that is the case, I believe the thing she should do is to leave her alcoholic husband, dissolve the marriage, and give him an opportunity to know the truth. An important part of that truth is his alcohol addiction and the trauma of divorce may help him to face up to it.

In most cases when this "noninterfering" argument is used, it denotes fear of losing the alcoholic to another, lack of faith in one's own worth as a partner in the marriage or, in more cases than not, a fear of unpleasantness, a fear of the strains, and a fear of the verbal violence and hostility that are likely to result when the problem is confronted openly. But isn't that better than later alcoholic death by violent accident, cirrhosis, or insanity?

Does an alcoholic or any person have a right to drink himself to death without being interfered with by another? Depending on one's feelings about liberty and license, particularly for the person "liberated" from the traditional Judaic-Christian view, arguments can be made for this kind of freedom. But I find it impossible to extend "sharing" in marriage to suicide pacts, especially if one partner loves life and wants to live. Marriages where one party does all the giving and sacrificing are rarely successful and happy.

Suppose this idea of giving the alcoholic the right to drink himself to death interferes with the rights of the co-alcoholic spouse. She is entitled to some help in keeping budgets, in making a living for the family, and in the parental responsibilities that alcoholics neglect frequently. Does the alcoholic's freedom to drink give him the freedom not to come to the table to eat, not to make a living, not to help rear the children, not to help in maintaining family relationships?

Let's stretch the point and say that it is the alcoholic's right to do as he sees fit as long as he brings home the paycheck and his wife is able to pay the bills. This isn't stretching things far, because it is precisely what millions of alcoholic wives are doing across the country. Doesn't the wife have an equal right to abandon this walking death scene? Doesn't she have a right to get away so she can rear the children better? If she has started footing the bills, as she frequently has to do, doesn't she have a right to refuse to support her alcoholic husband in his habit? Do not her rights include the right *not* to pay for his booze? Do not her rights include the right to leave him every time he passes out, abuses her, or neglects his personal hygiene? Where do her rights and duties begin in relation to his?

The answer is in the original proposition. If she loves him and he loves her, then she has a duty to try to learn how she can use guided intervention to bring him back to being the man she thought she was marrying or the man she may have married originally before alcohol changed him and his behavior.

If she finds that she truly does not love him, then I believe she owes it to herself first, to her children, and to her alcoholic mate to be truthful even if *he* cannot be. She should remove herself from his life and not continue to contribute to his problem with a tragic lie.

All persons married to alcoholics contribute to the problem. I have never known an alcoholic marriage in which the nonalcoholic spouse did not aggravate the problem. I am convinced that, unwittingly and with the best of intentions, every person married to an alcoholic I have ever met has made the alcoholic's problem worse and blocked the start of the recovery process.

If all wives of alcoholics (or husbands of alcoholics) unknowingly make the problem *worse*, how much worse must it be for the alcoholic whose spouse has a lover and is fighting guilt feelings? There are great ambivalences involved. Does not this alcoholic get more *harmful* consideration out of the guilt feelings of the unfaithful wife? Such a wife is afraid to get angry and rebel because of her own guilt feelings. Her final frightening solution is to *accept* his drinking and drunken behavior with seeming patience and no protest. Anger and rebellion would surely show more love.

Almost every alcoholic wants to feel drunk or be drunk most of the time. The unfaithful spouse can keep him quiet and satisfied simply by allowing him to drink without interference. Thus, she is aggravating his problem. But I believe that deep within, every alcoholic knows the bitter truth about what the alcohol is doing to him and he therefore knows that someone who allows him to drink without protest is allowing him to kill himself. A case referred to earlier makes the point. When the alcoholic husband found a bottle of whiskey on his breakfast table instead of eggs and bacon, he asked, "What are you trying to do, kill me?"

The alcoholic may suspect deep within that love is gone when someone accepts his excessive drinking. But he gets one of the things he is always looking for, a good excuse to continue drinking. Feeling and knowing he is unloved, he justifies the need for more drink.

But it is the loving, trying, sacrificing wife that guided intervention can help. With the rarest exceptions, without outside help, this same loving wife is worsening the problem of her alcoholic husband. How does she do it? First, she falls prey to some of the alcoholic's own delusions. Alcoholics usually deny that their problem is as bad as others say it is. They invent intricate rationalizations to explain their disorderly lives. Their wives frequently accept these defenses with the same fervor.

BLACKOUTS

Alcoholics have a highly developed memory for recalling all the pleasant things associated with drinking. They also are able to forget (black out) any memory of the most unpleasant consequences of their drinking experiences. To aid and abet this phenomenon is the additional effect of alcohol on many people called the blackout. Do not confuse this expression with "passing out" to unconsciousness. To black out in the alcoholism lexicon is merely to suffer temporary amnesia as a result of getting drunk. Most alcoholics when they get drunk also blackout. They cannot recall most of the things going on around them even though this impairment of awareness is not apparent to those around them. After a frightening drunken experience such as a bad automobile accident or a jail experience, alcoholics rarely remember any details. This is sometimes a never-ending source of irritation to wives who find it hard to believe that their alcoholic husbands cannot remember that most embarrassing of moments or most frightening of experiences in their lives. But it is frequently not exaggerated when the alcohol addict says he doesn't remember it "very well." He may not remember it at all and is tired of saying so to people who don't believe him.

Many wives tend to be protective of childish husbands. The wife of the alcoholic husband has more to protect. So she begins to accept his rationalizations, denials, and projections as her own. She joins him in recalling how pleasantly he behaved at the Joneses' cocktail party and how he did not get drunk on that occasion. ("Bill Jones actually drank much more.") She also tends to be one with him in forgetting the loss of the driver's license or the nightclub where he was asked to leave or had to be carried out.

When his drinking finally begins to reach the horrifying stages that are harder and harder to ignore, she does something ineffectual about it. She hides the bottles or pours the booze down the sink. These tactics have only a temporary effect, of course, and are not recommended by anyone who understands the problem. If an alcoholic makes up his mind that he is going to drink, a mere woman or man cannot stop him short of locking him up in a barren cell and posting a bribe-proof twenty-four-hour guard. Even that doesn't help much, because at the end of the incarceration, every alcoholic will get drunk before he does anything else (unless, it must be stated, a full plan of action has been formulated beforehand).

What happens over and over is that the wife tries a number of tactics. She threatens divorce or separation if he doesn't stop drinking. Sometimes for a short while this helps. The alcoholic does stop or slows down enough to meet her demands. She feels very happy about this, and he in turn is proud of himself. Having both partaken of some happiness and good feeling, then she cannot get quite as angry and upset the next time around when he gets drunk. After all, she can and does rationalize, he did stop for a while. That proves 1) he is not an alcoholic, 2) he really does care and does love me and the children, and 3) he is going to really quit someday as he says since he has shown he can do it. The next time he is drunk she is better prepared to live with it and goes about her business while his addiction problem is not only getting worse but has new reinforcement from her attitude.

Slowly, over the months and years, the wife of the alcoholic becomes a co-alcoholic, not a drinking victim but a victim of the delusions and games that alcoholism and marital interaction bring about. She too suffers from the defense mechanisms that protect the alcoholic from knowing the truth about himself. She too remembers the good things, the happy things about his drinking, and finds it easier and easier not to dwell on the tragic and bitter experiences.

The co-alcoholic can rationalize herself into believing that it isn't as bad as everyone seems to think. ("He's still holding his job, isn't he?" "He doesn't drink as much as some people, and he really isn't an 'alcoholic.' " "Who ever heard of an alcoholic as successful as he is in his work?") But none of these rationalizations will protect the sane person for long while pretending to have a normal home life while the walls are crumbling.

This is written to help these victims help their beloved alcoholics. It is written after many years of unplanned tests, many failures, and enough successes to have made it all worthwhile.

2

You Can't Stop Him But You Can Start Him

As the concerned person your goal must be to start your alcoholic on a program of recovery and to keep him there. It is not to stop his drinking. That is the alcoholic's decision to make and his alone. It is a misunderstanding of this goal that causes most failures with concerned persons of alcoholics. A majority mistakenly believe they have tried the guided intervention plan and that it has failed.

Several years ago a distraught wife called me late one night about her drunken husband. She was desperate and afraid. He could not stop drinking. His behavior was unpredictable and irrational. She made an appointment and came to see me the following morning and gave me the history. Her husband's problem had become critical only in the last four or five years. He had been to one treatment center for several weeks, twice. Once he had stayed sober about a month after leaving, the second time only one week. After discussing the case with her and explaining the principles of guided intervention, I recommended that he be sent to the same treatment center again for detoxication, three weeks of rest, and Alcoholics Anonymous programming.

After several days the alcohol was out of his system and his hands and spirits were steady. His wife and I went to see him. I explained my program to him. He listened and then turned to me and said, "In other words, the first time I start drinking again, you advise my wife to divorce me. Right?"

I replied that this was entirely wrong. "If you get on this program and stay with it," I told him, "I not only won't advise your wife to leave you if you start drinking again, I myself will come to your side to help you!"

I am sure this man did not believe me at the time. But he said he would do as his wife and I asked. And he did. For about two months he came to two group meetings a week and to as many private counseling sessions as we felt were needed. Then, as happens to most alcoholics, a so-called "slip" occurred. We do not call them slips but interruptions—interruptions of sobriety—thereby not establishing a blame or an excuse but merely acknowledging a happening. Sobriety has been interrupted.

This interruption was serious. My client was very drunk and could not stop drinking. His wife agreed to have him hospitalized under a physician's care for detoxicating. His doctor and I tried to get him a room. The hospital was full and we had to wait. Meanwhile, his situation was not getting better. An alcoholic trying to withdraw from alcohol after a prolonged drunken period is a frightening and tragic figure. A day and a half passed while we waited. His wife called me again and said she was afraid he would get in his car and drive to a liquor store for more booze and that he might have a serious accident. What should she do? I decided to do something very risky. I told her I would come to see him and since we were not able to get him hospitalized immediately, I would bring him some whiskey to avoid the dreaded delirium tremens (DTs) until he could be hospitalized. (I do not recommend this.) I picked up a fifth and drove out to their home. I left the bottle in my car and went in to see the sick man. Alone with him in his den, I told him how sorry I was to find him so sick, which he truly was. I told him I wanted to help him in any way I could. What could I do for him?

He looked at me and said, "Do you really mean it? Do you really want to help me?"

I repeated my concern for him with all the earnestness I could show. "All right," he said. "If you really want to know what I need, I'll tell you. I need a drink!" He was sure that he was wasting his time, but he was desperate enough to try anything.

"Okay," I said, "I have a bottle in the car I brought for you. I'll get it."

His amazement and surprise knew no bounds. "Hey, wait a minute," he said. "Maybe that's not what I ought to have. That's really the last thing I should have, isn't it?" He seemed to be pleading with me to disagree with him, which I did. I then brought him the bottle and asked him to take it very slowly—to make it last until the next day when he would be getting into the hospital. He agreed and he kept his promise. The next day he entered the hospital for detoxicating. We had many problems with this man afterward. But they were medical, and he never again touched alcohol. Now it has been more than five years since that last drinking episode.

I have narrated this to make my point more easily remembered. It is obvious to anyone who learns much about guided intervention that giving the alcoholic alcohol is not a part of the plan. We never help an alcoholic get alcohol. I hasten to say that I would not again take whiskey to an alcoholic even about to go into delirium tremens as this client was. Instead I would remember that an intravenous tranquilizer is available from almost any doctor or emergency room of most general hospitals. That would be less likely to cause the patient to continue drinking.

There was a second reason for taking the alcohol to that suffering man that day. I wanted to communicate to him—on an emotional level—that I knew how he was suffering, that I loved him and wanted to help him. My giving him a drink that day told him as no words could that I was sympathetic to his suffering. He received the message. From that day on, he knew that I was his friend and not someone simply trying to deny him alcohol or threaten him into not drinking at the risk of losing his wife. But loving wives of suffering alcoholics usually don't need to go to such extremes. Usually they have communicated this love, in this way, several times too often. In their desperation, wives of alcoholics usually run the gamut of everything that might possibly help. Recently a wife of an alcoholic to whom I was trying to explain guided intervention said to me: "But I've done everything for him that I could possibly do." When I asked her what were some of the things she had done, she mentioned nursing him and helping him to get over his heavy drinking episodes. This kind of help is traditional in our culture and it is usually unavoidable. But it is not the kind of help to use in guided intervention without first becoming fully aware of the certain consequences it will have. There are alternatives to consider also.

The principles of guided intervention are rarely used because they are not at all obvious. When one tries to think of analogies one might say they are like the advice given to golfers: Keep your eye on the ball; don't worry about the fairway or the green up ahead. But *before* you can get a golf ball into the air you must hit it with the club, and to hit it it is necessary to look at it the moment the club comes down upon it. That is easy to follow for its logic is obvious. It is not as obvious to explain that an alcoholic will not really stop drinking until he gets into treatment. For one thing, the alcoholic is always there to tell you otherwise. Yet it is true. The number of alcoholics who become total abstainers without outside help is infinitesimal. I know none. The reason revolves around the definition of alcoholism. In my definition of alcoholism, self-recovery is unknown. If a heavy drinker and frequent drunkard stops drinking, we can very well be assured he was not a true chronic alcoholic. Any wife of a frequent drunkard can apply this criterion very simply by determining whether he can stop alone or not. I would guess that by the third time a suspected subject has seriously promised to stop drinking or drastically reduce his consumption and failed, he has shown he is a chronic alcoholic. That means he is not likely to make it without outside help. This guideline applies even to drinkers who do manage not to drink for periods as long as six months, twelve months, or even longer.

The co-alcoholic who plans to apply guided intervention must remember the rule of the golfer: Keep your eye on the ball, not on the fairway. Keep your eye on getting him started in treatment, *not* on getting him to stop drinking. You must not judge him as much on whether he continues drinking, as you will learn when following the program, but on *how* he responds to the entire program.

There are many sound reasons for this. The most important is that it is practically impossible to help him by issuing ultimatums about what you are going to do if he does not stop drinking. Successful loan companies never discuss beforehand how diligently they pursue the slow-paying customers or those who don't or cannot pay what they owe. Pleasant, sweet-tasting children's laxatives were invented to take the place of castor oil and other bitter ones. Finally, the intelligent concerned person should never forget: The most threatening thing anyone can say to an alcoholic is: "Don't drink, you can't have any more!"

The chronic alcoholic is almost always going to be either a gamma or a delta alcoholic under the classifications of Dr. E. M. Jellinek, a universally respected authority. A *gamma* is a binge drinker who starts drinking, gets drunk, and cannot stop without great pain and trouble. A *delta* is one who stays a little drunk almost all the time, sipping his alcohol from morning to night, always being assured that there is a supply handy for his hourly needs. Apparently the most common American alcoholic is the gamma type. Jellinek found that the vast majority of members of Alcoholics Anonymous were gammas. To either one—gamma or delta—the ugliest and most frightening threat that can be made is to suggest that he will have to do without alcohol. That will discourage him and is usually much more harmful than helpful to the goal.

The gamma alcoholic can put up with a great many discomforts for a reasonable length of time as long as he knows that there is going to be a drink at the end of the period. In persuading alcoholics to accept an experimental kind of treatment, some researchers have employed this knowledge to win volunteers by promising a drinking experience at the conclusion of the experimental period. Knowing, after all the unpleasantness of the experimental period, that he will get a chance for blessed relief with alcohol, the alcoholic can endure long periods of abstinence. It works because he knows it won't last forever.

The same knowledge is employed in the famous twenty-four-hour system used by members of Alcoholics Anonymous. A true AA disciple never says he is not going to drink again for the rest of his life or even for another week or month. He says instead, "I'm not going to have a drink for the next twenty-four hours." The AA logic behind this states that, although it might be well-nigh impossible for an alcoholic to stop drinking forever, any fool can stay sober for one day. And, of course, it is true. But another way of stating it is to say, "Well, I may need a drink pretty soon. In fact, I know I will. But I am going to put it off for twenty-four hours."

Many members of AA have had to employ the "twenty-four-hour system" on a twenty-four-minute or five-minute basis when they were struggling to withdraw after a binge. They found they could not control their desire to have a drink immediately if they were thinking in terms of a lifetime or even a month or a week. That would be too much pain and suffering rolled into one moment to be endurable. But they could pass up the drink for a short time if they were telling their feeling selves (their unconscious) that the possibility of taking a drink later was still an option.

Under the guided intervention technique, the co-alcoholic or concerned person cannot and must not try to tell the alcoholic what he is going to do or not to do. She must never tell the alcoholic that he must quit drinking. How much less acceptable can an ugly threat be coming from his wife when it is so unbearable that he is afraid to say it to himself? Why should anyone try to force a painful and unbearable idea on any person which that person cannot bring himself to entertain even momentarily? It may be a farfetched analogy, but how many of us have really ever tried to imagine what kind of pain and suffering is endured in hell? Or, even in a house fire? Why is it that we must be forced to discuss the death of our loved ones? None of us likes to even *think* about such pain and suffering. It is unnatural to accept such thoughts for long, and most of us have to be persuaded to sit down and discuss such matters. But even then we rarely indulge in letting it sink in. We refuse to admit to ourselves that we are talking about our dear, loved ones actually being dead, buried, six feet under, gone forever. That is why it doesn't make sense to try to help an alcoholic by beginning with the dictum, "You've got to stop drinking!" As soon as you say that, you have lost your chances of communicating. As soon as you utter the unspeakable words, the alcoholic tunes you out and says to himself, even unconsciously, "She doesn't know what she's asking of me. I can't survive without it!" I shall discuss elsewhere some of the feelings and emotions of the alcoholic. For now I'll stay with the subject of *not* approaching your alcoholic with this most dreaded of all ideas. Let's take a clue from the experimental researchers who promised a drinking experience when their work was done. Let's also take a clue from the thousands of AA who will tell you that the twenty-four hours at a time way is the *only* way to quit. It works for thousands of AAs who use it. I firmly believe it is the most wise counsel in the early days of abstinence for alcoholics.

We know that an alcoholic must eventually quit before he can recover, you might want to remind me. Yes, that's true. We also know he knows it as well as you do. That also is true. But it is not necessary that the truth must always be put into words. This is especially the case when you are dealing with a problem that requires you to curtail your behavior, your thinking, and your attitudes. It can also be said that death is inevitable. We will all die. But it is considered sick and undesirable constantly to talk about it, especially dwelling on the sad and ugly side of it. When you are wise and mature you accept the inevitability of death as you accept the inevitability of old age, although you may not find it necessary to talk about it very often. What you do like to talk of often is growing and laughing and having good times with good friends and good food and happy experiences. When you must talk about other things, such as your daily routine and your livelihood, if you are wise and mature, you do so with frankness and you emphasize the happier side.

The alcoholic knows that whatever he does to recover from

alcoholism is invariably going to mean giving up the alcohol. Sometimes, I have found, the alcoholic accepts the program just because he is able to persuade himself that he is *not* going to be obliged to give up his drinking. This doesn't work for long, but sometimes of his own volition the alcoholic gets himself started this way. It isn't too far removed from the AA twenty-four-hour plan or the researcher's promised drinking experience technique. But most alcoholics know that total abstinence is the goal of the recovery process as it is in guided intervention. Those who want less than total abstinence should look elsewhere. Moderate drinking for alcoholics is not a part of our plan.

It is with this thought in your mind—firmly placed and not to be dislodged—that you must implement guided intervention. *Your* goal—the co-alcoholic's goal—is not to get your alcoholic husband to stop drinking. He will have to make that decision himself. *You* cannot make it for him. Your goal is that he *do* something. Your goal is that he *go* to a meeting. *Go* to an appointment. *Take* a medicine. (More about that later.) *Go* to see a certain person. It is always that he *do* something. It is never that he *not* do something. You can never know that a person is *not* doing something.

I remember in the early days of counseling I would ask one of my alcoholic friends what his plans were. Invariably, he would tell me that he planned to "quit drinking." That was his goal, he would say. I would reply that his goal was unacceptable, that it wouldn't work. "Draw me a picture of it," I would challenge. "How can you draw a picture of a man *not* drinking?" It is, of course, impossible. Any attempt to draw a picture of a person *not* doing anything must result in a picture of a person *doing* something. So it is with trying to get someone to stop drinking. You cannot draw a picture of your goal for them until you draw a picture of what you want them to do. There just isn't any other way of showing them what *not* to do.

3

How to Start

Any active alcoholic—even one who has never admitted to the problem—can be turned around and started on a program of recovery by his wife. It is really simple. It is as simple as what you do to lose weight: You eat less. That's all. Do that and you'll lose weight without fail. But how hard that simple rule is to put into practice. Very few people succeed. Those who do succeed do so with help and expert knowledge applied at a favorable time and under the right circumstances.

To call guided intervention simple is just as misleading as the rule for losing weight. To be honest, it is even harder. It is much harder. I make the comparison because the principles of guided intervention sound simple, so simple as to mislead.

If you try to apply them and fail, it may be because you are unable to bridge the chasm—that big, wide canyon between saying and doing—and you may want to give up. But continue undaunted. Overweight people have found many answers to their problem. One of the newer ones is the organization of Weight Watchers. It seems to me that the most important factor in the success of Weight Watchers is the encouragement and help that fat people get from other people. Outside help and reinforcement is needed. It can even be the vital ingredient of success. I recommend that before you try to implement guided intervention that you get outside help and reinforcement. With someone to counsel and encourage you, your task will be easier and more likely to be successful. Your guide will be this book together with your counselor.

In addition to getting outside help, you should also have a *feeling*-level understanding of alcoholism. This means not only to understand alcoholism in your head at a conscious level but also to understand it in "the pit of your stomach." It is what therapists call gut level. You will also need to have a "feeling level" as well as an intellectual understanding of yourself and particularly an understanding of how you react to alcoholism and your alcoholic. I suggest that you read the chapter on this understanding process (chapter 11) and some of the books I recommend. You may be able to read them and start your guided intervention program simultaneously. On the other hand, you may feel a need to accomplish these changes in attitude before you start. I suggest you discuss it with your counselor after you have chosen one. You may already be saturated with information and feeling-level understanding of alcoholism and your alcoholic. You may be ready to start with the ABCs of guided intervention. In either case I see no reason to put off an explanation of the procedures. Knowing them in advance may help you to keep going.

The first thing is to choose your counselor. My experience prior to writing this book has involved me or a member of my staff as a guide. But I have also counseled concerned persons of alcoholics from my home in Nashville in places as far away as San Francisco, New York City, Mississippi, and Florida by telephone and letter. And I have worked with the co-alcoholic in person without the alcoholic. In three out of four cases the alcoholics responded to the treatment-by-proxy by abstaining and getting into a program. These experiences encouraged me to write a book that might help others succeed without my direct involvement.

A person to advise and reinforce you is so important that I suggest that you should not start applying the program until you have obtained one. Preferably this person needs to be someone experienced in dealing successfully with alcoholics. My first choice would be a professional alcoholism counselor. As this is written a movement is under way across the United States to set up standards for certifying alcoholism counselors. They will be known as certified alcoholism (or addiction) counselors. If these certified counselors are available, one of them should be your choice to guide you in implementing the intervention program in this book. You should, of course, also continue direct reference to the book.

My second suggestion is imperative: This person should read the book. Lend him your copy if need be after you have read it. Then you must ascertain that he reach the same conclusion that you have reached. If you both agree that the plan of finding a dependable, attainable, tangible alternative to active alcoholism can be started with guided intervention, then you should be ready to apply it forthwith.

Determine if a certified alcoholism counselor or the equivalent, an alcoholism counselor with at least two years of experience in counseling alcoholics (not in mental health, marriage counseling, or anything else), is available. If there isn't an acceptable alcoholism counselor available, then find either a member of Alcoholics Anonymous or a member of Al-Anon. Ask this person to read this book. Again this person must be in agreement about these matters. When you find him or her accept his (or her) guidance.

If neither an AA member nor a member of Al-Anon is available to you (and sometimes one of them can be hard to find in spite of their great numbers) I suggest as your third choice a social worker or other professional guidance counselor, a marriage counselor, your own minister, your doctor if he will give you the time, or some other experienced and wise person. I would avoid close friends or kin. Following the foregoing priorities, the next most important consideration is that this person be in agreement with the principles of this book. I don't think you will find serious disagreement. The third consideration should be this person's maturity, wisdom, and compassion.

In getting help from an AA member or a member of Al-Anon, avoid those persons who believe that *only* an alcoholic can help another alcoholic, and that the AA way to recovery is the *only* way. You already should know to avoid that person who tells you that you must "wait until he hits bottom" to help your alcoholic. As I have already noted, that is frequently much too long. The alcoholic may die. Sometimes hitting his bottom means merely coming to that point in which *you* (not he) scream "no more!" As for the idea that only an alcoholic can help another alcoholic, let me say that an alcoholic who has suffered through and recovered may have some advantages over someone speaking from vicarious experience but sometimes he has disadvantages. His total personality or drinking history may be so different from your alcoholic's that you can both be easily mislead. Literary critics have said that Stephen Crane's *Red Badge of Courage* is one of the best fictional accounts ever written about the ravages of war. Yet Crane was never in a battle or even in the army. Some excellent marriage counselors (notably Catholic priests) have never been married. And does anyone question the expertise of a male obstetrician because he has never had a baby?

Alcoholics Anonymous, its worldwide fellowship, and the great Twelve Steps* are *almost* indispensable to any alcoholic. The AA movement deserves at least half or even more of the credit for starting professional alcoholism research and treatment in the United States. It also can lay claim to more recoveries than any other. But it is not the only way. As for what is the best way, I can only say that to a man saved from death by a second-rate physician, that physician is the greatest. And for the person who finds recovery in AA, it is the best way. Baptists who reach their reward in heaven are sure theirs was the one true religion. But what are those Methodists, Episcopalians, Jews, Catholics, Presbyterians, agnostics

*The text of the Steps and some interpretation is found in chapter 10, pp. 137.

and others doing there? I know many recovered alcoholics who have refused to get into AA. But I still think it is unwise. Some people may get to heaven without ever joining a church, but I do not recommend that either.

This is one of the most important projects of your life so you must choose your helper with utmost care. Look at that person's intimate life as well as his public image. Is he reasonably happy? Is he successful? Not necessarily financially, but does he seem to be satisfied with his life and the standard of living he has? Is your selection a person who is constantly attacking and finding fault with others? Is he or she a person whose life seems to be exaggerated in any department? I urge you to shun the religious fanatic as well as the AA fanatic. Pass up the excessive extrovert, a person who seems compulsively driven to being with several people all the time, or the excessive introvert, a person who shuns almost all social contacts. The opinions of these people would be warped, prejudiced, and misleading. It should go without saying that if he is an AA member, he should have at least two or three years of uninterrupted sobriety. If one is a member of Al-Anon—it is likely to be a wife—her alcoholic should have about that same length of sobriety. If the person you select disagrees with the principles of guided intervention, ask him to give you an alternative. Does he or she know something better? I daresay he will not. The alternative to guided intervention is frequently help for the concerned person alone and abandonment of the alcoholic on the grounds that he is not "ready." It is your job to get him ready. Some people will find some legitimate disagreements with some point or other in this book with good cause. But this should not be cause to reject the basic proposition of the book, that it may very well be in your power to get your alcoholic into treatment. Do not be distracted from that.

I am not advising you of anything I do not believe and practice. Therefore, I am going to do everything I can to convince you of its wisdom, and at the same time try to be as honest and straightforward as I can.

So, now you have chosen your guide, he or she has read the book, and you have both agreed that it is time to start. Let's get on with it.

Guided intervention assumes that the co-alcoholic loves

her alcoholic and that she is loved in return. It also assumes that the alcoholic cannot therefore live without the co-alcoholic any more than the co-alcoholic feels that she wants to live without him.

These assumptions then are going to be applied in a way to give the alcoholic a choice: Either he begins to do some of the things that are helpful to recovery from alcoholism or he is going to start losing you, his wife. Eventually, it must become increasingly clear to him (if he fights it for long) that he will lose you forever. Remember you are offering him a simple dependable, attainable, tangible alternative, not to stop drinking but to do something so he won't lose you. Drinking is not the no-no. The only no-no is not keeping up the therapeutic activity you have urged, whether it is going to a counselor, to AA, or to someone else.

The idea of losing you from his life forever may never have to be spoken and will probably never happen. But you *must* be prepared to carry this plan to its logical conclusion if necessary. You must be able to say to yourself: "I love my husband enough to give him up forever if that is the only way I can find to make him wake up to the fact that he is killing himself with my help."

This is the essence of guided intervention. Until you can sincerely say that and mean it, you should not undertake it. At this point I will assume that you can and do say it.

This plan involves an ultimatum; it involves implied force. It is not unlike a method called "constructive coercion." But if it is coercion it is coercion that starts with a feather touch to the arm instead of a two-by-four on the head. Guided intervention does not rule out the two-by-four completely because some alcoholics won't understand feather touches, elbow nudging, strong words, or anything else. But the co-alcoholic using guided intervention probably won't find it necessary to use a two-by-four if she is wise and faithful in using the procedures suggested here.

Even before the alcoholic is given the feather touch, there has to be a preliminary quieting of the atmosphere. The alcoholic is going to notice an absence of nagging, crying, threatening, and screaming. He will also not hear or see any more whiskey being poured down the sink, hidden, or given away.

No longer is he going to hear long sermons. He also is not going to hear any more empty threats to move, divorce him, separate, or call the police, because the first thing the co-alcoholic does is to stop all these activities.

When your alcoholic drinks and it is too hard for you to take, go to another room or leave the house. But do not fuss or nag about it. "Why not?–if I'm really interested in getting him to stop drinking," you may ask. Because it does more harm than good. He is more likely to keep drinking if you protest than he is if you are quiet. "Oh, but you don't know my husband," I can hear you saying, "if I shut up he's going to drink and drink and drink. That's all he wants me to do. Shut up and let him get drunk." Okay, this may be true in the beginning. It might be true for a while. But there is a greater probability that if there is any chance at all that he will ever stop, it will be when he makes the decision (or thinks he does) all by himself. And even if he doesn't stop, at least there is more quiet around the house. But I am only at the beginning, in the preliminary stage.

Still in this preliminary stage you will also avoid discussions about his drinking, and about his failures that are connected or even that might be connected to his drinking. This means that you will avoid censoring him for *anything* at all. If he doesn't go to church with you, don't fuss about it. If he won't agree to having friends over for a social gathering (particularly nondrinkers), don't press the matter. If he refuses to accept other social invitations or even so much as take you to a movie, live with this for the time being. There is much more at stake than this temporary inconvenience.

In this preliminary quieting of the atmosphere, the rule is stop nagging, fussing, and acting out in any way or about anything connected with his drinking in the past or in the future. Don't find any fault with him for anything because chances are it is either connected with his drinking or he will see it as being related.

Now comes the actual touching with the feather. Now you are going to do something positive. It may not seem like much, and it will vary in the degree of its trauma for each alcoholic. For one it may be one of the biggest shocks of his life. For another it may draw only a lifted eyebrow. But, if it is done right, you may be sure it will be felt much more than a lifted eyebrow would indicate.

This positive step—this feather touch—is simply an announcement: You announce to your alcoholic that *you* are going to do—or have already done—something about *your* problem.

This action has to be a dependable, attainable, and tangible alternative to whatever has been going on before. It is going to be a simple announcement such as "Honey, I have something important to say to you. I am going to a meeting of Alcoholics Anonymous tonight. Do you want to go with me?" You, a nonalcoholic, can go to any meeting of AA that is not for alcoholics only. Just be sure it is an open meeting that anyone can attend. In almost any city or town in the United States there are such meetings, and they can be found under AA or Alcoholics Anonymous in the telephone directory.

In one of our outpatient counseling programs called Azalea Center we usually use the conference with the center counselor as the first step. "Darling, I have something important to tell you. I have an appointment to see an alcoholism counselor at Azalea Center at 10 o'clock tomorrow. Do you want to go with me?"

You must deliver this short statement when the alcoholic is sober, calm, and in a peaceful frame of mind. Instead of calling him by his name, you should use "Honey," "Baby," "Daddy," "Darling," or your most endearing term for him, if that is your style. Your words should be as natural and as serious as you can make them. The best time to deliver your message might be in the morning while both of you are still in the bedroom or when his shaving has begun. The alcoholic should be as awake and as alert as he can be. Some people are never alert at that hour of the morning. And some alcoholics start drinking before they get up. They start with secret trips to the kitchen or the basement or the car. But you must start at all costs, and the excuse that there isn't a good time cannot be valid for long. Everybody is sometimes awake and reasonably sober.

In making your announcement you should remember what to avoid. The importance of remembering these things cannot be overemphasized. Above all, you are not to try to persuade your alcoholic to accompany you wherever you are going. You are simply announcing that you are going and are opening the door for him to go with you if *he* wants to. But to try to persuade, threaten, or preach at this point will not do any good. On the contrary, to use pressure will more than likely do harm. ("Oh, brother!" I can hear some of you saying, "what he doesn't know about my husband!" And I reply, "Trust me.") The idea is merely to state the case, to make it hard to ignore by opening with a preliminary announcement, "I have something important to tell you," and to make certain that he hears it. Once that is done, most of the benefit you are going to get has already come even if you cannot recognize it.

To some alcoholic husbands this is not going to come as a surprise, especially if you have already been to AA, alone or with him, Al-Anon, or a counselor. But more probably than not, unless you are currently pursuing one of these activities, it is going to surprise him. If you have never done any of these things, it will be a bigger surprise. It may also be more. It may very well be a traumatic experience for him. If carried out correctly, he will have noticed the preliminary quieting of the atmosphere. He is going to notice that you have quit nagging, fussing, crying, screaming, and trying to stop him from drinking, as well as sermonizing him about his failings, his bad habits, neglect of the family, and other things. He may not acknowledge it to you, but you can be certain if it is a big change in your behavior (and it usually is), he has noticed it. He may even have moderated his drinking because of it.

In some cases he may have actually stopped drinking for a day or two or even longer. This is not to be taken as a sign that he is going to solve his problem alone. Do not return to your old ways because he stops or slows down on his consumption. This is a temporary reaction and cannot *under any circumstances* be viewed as anything else. To think it is the beginning of an actual abstinence program is to underestimate the seriousness of alcohol addiction. There is still a very hard, long effort ahead, and it is going to take a long time.

To some alcoholic husbands this announcement of your

decision to do something positive (and as he is to discover, you are going to act either with him or without him) is going to be a shock. Your alcoholic is probably living in a state of depression. He has slowly gotten to such a low point of self-esteem that he hates himself most of his waking hours. He hasn't told you that, and he may never be able to tell you or anyone else. But it is nonetheless true. So he discovers by your announcement that his state of alcoholism that he secretly realizes is ruining his life has become so obvious to you that you have decided to go out and do something about it on your own.

It should be reiterated that the announcement should not under any circumstances be made unless you, the co-alcoholic, are positively going to do what you say you are going to do. Not to do it is to weaken your chances of helping your alcoholic for the present and in the future. If you haven't made a firm decision to follow through, do not make the announcement.

There are four ways the alcoholic husband may respond to your announcement. The first one is with open, loud hostility.

"You did what? What the hell for? Why do *you* want to go to such a thing? I thought you said I was the one with the problem!" And, of course, on and on, much more and more hostile. There are many possible hostile responses that can come from him. All that needs to be said here is that you should not respond with hostility in return or even to respond at all except to accept the hostility quietly and, if necessary, respond very firmly, quietly, and with assurance, "Okay, I'll go by myself." Or, you might say, "Okay, that's your decision."

The "that's your decision" response is one that should be *remembered*. It can be used frequently and effectively. One of the alcoholic's common manipulations that can be put off with "it's your decision" is the one in which the alcoholic says he drinks because you nagged him into it or because you made him upset about something or other. He had to drink to get over it. By saying "it's your decision," you refuse to fight and you also refuse to assume the responsibility of trying to stop him from drinking or of trying to make him do anything. He cannot very well (although he may anyway!) blame you for forcing him if you make it clear that it is his decision to do whatever he does.

The second way the alcoholic may respond to the announcement is practically to ignore it by seeming not to take it seriously or by refusing to respond to it at all. I believe the best way to handle this kind of passive response is with passivity in return. A long moment of silence carries a tremendous message. It can be heard as a variety of thoughts by your alcoholic. It can mean "She's going to go and there's nothing I can do to stop her." It can mean "Damn her! She's going to start that kind of thing again. Well, I'm not even going to discuss it with her. I'll show her!" But it doesn't matter. Your silence in return merely will confirm his worst suspicions, and as long as you are sure he heard you, you should not even repeat it. Remember, you announced that it was important before you said it, so the chances that he did not hear it are remote.

The third way he may respond is by the masterful manipulation that so many alcoholics know. That is, he may pretend serious interest. He might get you to talk about it, ask you questions, and give you a qualified answer to the question part that sounds better than it is:

"Oh, I don't know. I guess going with you wouldn't do any harm. When did you say it was again?"

But this response should be taken with a large grain of salt. The chances are that he is not going to find the time to go at all. If he's the masterful manipulator he seems to be, he has learned never to fight the inevitable—which in this case is the announcement. But he will dodge the issue. This response is the one you should dislike the most, because it is a sign your alcoholic is going to be hard to handle. Either one of the first two responses is better because both of them tell you your alcoholic has been reached. You have hit him with something he finds hard to handle. You have offered him the help he wants but is afraid to accept. The fact that he fights it, either openly or passively, is a sure sign of deep respect for the idea. It usually means that he is taking it to his breast for study and meditation. You must always keep this in mind. Your alcoholic husband has received the announcement but may never mention it again. But it has probably registered with him with the permanency of a hot branding iron on his chest. You should not forget that.

The fourth response is the one you really least expect, and yet the one that happens much more frequently than you might think. This is the honest, the interested response, the one you dreamed about. Yes, he'll go. He thinks he might get something out of it. What do you do then? One thing you must do is to avoid overreacting. Show you are pleased with him in a quiet friendly way. But avoid histrionics. Avoid tears. Avoid a long speech. Don't even act too excited. Calm down. One thing to remember is that your alcoholic is probably having a more difficult time emotionally than you are. So be glad. Smile. But don't fail to stay calm and cool. Try to handle it the way you would respond to any other pleasant plan to go somewhere. "Okay, we'll eat supper a little early and take the Ford." Make whatever appropriate statement fits the occasion. Once that is done, if he doesn't pursue the subject, drop it.

There are a variety of other possibilities, of course. He may prefer to go alone. He may even be very willing to go but not be able to go at the time you have planned. Be careful how you handle it, but don't make it hard for him to accept. Help him in every way you can. If he prefers to go alone, accept that. If he wants to go with someone else, say an older son or recovering alcoholic friend or anyone else, agree to it. When an alcoholic agrees to take the first step toward accepting help for his problem, it could be a moment that may not recur for a long time. Use it. Help him. Don't do anything to make it hard for him. Remember it isn't easy for him to say yes, to say he's ready to go. So take him at his word. Be receptive and be calm.

Another thing, don't try to rush him. If you had planned the event for a week away, don't suddenly decide that since he's willing you will now make it today or tomorrow. All such reactions on your part are likely to frighten him.

If this is your first experience with this kind of reaction, accept almost any unusual or inconvenient proposal that he might attach to his agreement. If he is agreeing to see an alcoholism counselor for the first time, it might be late at night or very early in the morning, a Sunday, or Christmas day. If it is, and he says he would like to talk right then and there, follow up immediately and see if the counselor can see you both then. Or him alone, if that's his preference. In my counseling work I have always had the rule that when an alcoholic was ready for the *first* counseling session my time was his time, be it the middle of the night, a holiday, or a vacation. (Not for a *drunk* alcoholic, mind you, and not twice in a row. But for the first vital interview, yes.) I believe many other professional alcoholism counselors will agree with that. And I know many AA members who do what is known as Twelfth Step work must often do it at odd hours. (Twelfth Step work usually means visiting an alcoholic in trouble, or in the words of the Step, "carrying the message" of AA.)

The general idea of the way to act after this happy response from your alcoholic is to be pleasing and affirmative, to accept his conditions and his wishes, and not to push, urge, cajole, or rush.

He may ask you questions. Many times these questions are a disguised manipulation. The best advice for handling them is to keep your answers brief and honest. Some examples might go like this:

"Say, just what does an alcoholism counselor do? Are they anything like psychiatrists?"

Answer: "I don't really know, but I guess we'll find out."

Question: "Why did you make an appointment for yourself? I'd think I was the only one who needed to see somebody like that."

Answer: "Well, the truth is *I* need some help myself. And I'm going to get it."

Question: "I've always heard that nobody can be helped unless he's ready to admit he's an alcoholic and stops drinking. And I'm not doing that. So what would be the point in going?" (This could be sincere, but this kind of half-negative question needs to be handled with care. It might be a manipulation, the opening wedge of another argument about his drinking. Don't get hooked.)

Answer: "I really don't know, for sure, But I'd like to find out."

Or, another answer: "Maybe so. Maybe you are not ready and will never admit you've got a problem. But I certainly have. I know *I* need some help. Maybe I'm the crazy one!" And, of course, you as a co-alcoholic are very likely suffering some of the same delusions and unrealistic attitudes as your alcoholic. You are probably just a little bit crazy at times as a result of your shared problem. So don't be afraid to say so. Just don't place any more blame on your alcoholic.

Or, if your planned first step was to go to an AA meeting, he might say: "Aren't you afraid people are going to see us there?"

Answer: "Well, *maybe* but *I'm* ready to take my chances. I've got to find some help for myself."

Any one or a variation of these replies to his response can be used. The idea is to avoid a long discussion. Avoid opinions and predictions, speculations and promises. Just decide to go, try to let him decide if he wants to go too, and then drop the subject. Don't mention it another time until it is necessary in the ordinary course of events when the time comes to leave.

Many alcoholics will also promise to go and then back down at the last minute. This, too, needs to be accepted gracefully. Let him know you are disappointed but don't get angry and above all don't preach. Don't make any veiled threats, sarcastic remarks, or even slam the door or walk heavily. You may let him know you are disappointed, but that's all. You say, "Well, I'm sorry you're not feeling well." Or, "I'm sorry you've changed your mind." Or, "I'm sorry you feel that way." And then leave for the meeting, the appointment, or whatever it was just as you had planned. Do not back down. Do not be discouraged. You will succeed eventually if you will follow directions.

4

Meeting Strong Resistance

Before discussing more phases of guided intervention after the preliminary quieting of the house and the initial announcement has been made, it is necessary to stop and consider that you may have run into strong resistance. Many wives of alcoholics who have so far been able to follow the intervention plan have been pleasantly and even shockingly surprised at the response they have had. It is an amazing thing to discover sometimes that an alcoholic is only a person waiting to be handled perceptively. Sometimes he will do the simple, commonsense thing if we just ask him in the right way. But then there are many who resist; many who are master manipulators and who are determined not to be guided into treatment. If you have not succeeded, let's consider some follow-ups for the hard-core addict.

That's what he is: a hard-core addict, not just a stubborn man. The real reason for his resistance is not that he doesn't like to be "manipulated." The true cause of his resistance is his terrible crying need for that continuing relief from his depression (psychic pain of the worst kind) that—he deeply believes—only his alcohol can bring. He is terribly frightened because you have threatened his dream world—his haven.

There are several things that can happen after you have repeated the feather-touch announcement over a short period of time as it should be. The average time should be about four weeks. Let us consider the dynamics of responses over a period of four weeks when your alcoholic is resisting and continues to say no.

You should be proceeding in the following fashion. After having made your initial announcement and been rejected, ignored, tricked, or outmaneuvered in some other way, start planning your follow-ups. The follow-up is essentially the same as the first announcement. You may ask, why not increase the pressure? Why wait? And the answer is that you *are* increasing the pressure just by continuing the phase. This is the most effective kind of increased pressure. It is merely to continue turning the screw without letting up on the pressure. Isn't your alcoholic going to be able to ignore this plan if you don't do something extra? Isn't he going to conclude he has nothing to worry about, that you're just doing some of the things you have been doing before? No, he is not going to see it that way because it isn't that way. This is a different time. This is a guided intelligent approach, well planned and coordinated.

You must continue to avoid all talk about alcoholism, his bad habits, his dangerous drinking behavior, his lack of understanding and consideration for you and the children, his endangering of his job, and so on.

You must also continue *not* to pour his booze down the sink, hide it, or get angry when he leaves to get a drink or goes to the liquor store or to the corner market for beer. You can and you do leave the room or leave the house but very quietly and without making a scene—if the drinking is more than you can take. But when you come back, you should again make it a point not to talk about it. Your guiding rule is: Don't talk about his bad habits, drinking, or anything related, and don't fuss or nag.

Now you have been to your first interview with the alcoholism counselor or to your first AA or Al-Anon meeting. The chances are that you feel encouraged and more determined than ever to follow through. Having met other alcoholics' wives whose husbands have stopped drinking and alcoholics whose wives are now happy, you may feel elated and optimistic. But then you get home and find that your own alcoholic is still oblivious of this other world of sober alcoholics, happy husbands, and happy wives. There he is, absolutely unchanged and unmindful of the rest of the world except his "drinkee," his "little beer," his "little bourbon," "relaxer," "toddy," or whatever other name he has for it. Sometimes, there is no name for the liquor itself. It's just "watching television," which in ten years hasn't ever happened without alcohol for companionship. Or it may be what he euphemistically refers to as "being myself," "getting a slight buzz," or "hell, just doing some drinking. What's wrong with that? I'm not hurting anyone else, am I?"

But whatever it is and whatever it is called, there is no apparent change. He seems not to have heard the first announcement after you had put your hopes in it so strongly, with faith and determination. So, maybe by now you would like to tell me: "You don't know my husband. He's not going to quit until the day he dies, and I am not sure he won't be drinking on that last day, too."

There is another kind of argument that needs to be met for the wife who gives up or has been outmaneuvered. You may say to yourself, "My Jim is different. He has always run the show. He has always been able to get his way with me, and there is no way I could outfox him. So, I may as well forget about it."

I would accept this argument more often and much easier for many wives who have said it to me except for one thing. Many of them have finally left their alcoholic husbands with divorces and without divorces. And even then many have continued to be outmaneuvered by an alcoholic husband to his tragic detriment. He has lost the wife as a wife but has been able to get drunk again and again with the help of a woman whose life has also been ruined, who has nothing but an illusion to live for, and whose illusion is weak and transitory. What a tragedy!

Other wives who left their husbands and divorced them and made whole new lives—with or without new mates for themselves—have found some happiness or even much happiness. But what about their alcoholic? Should we abandon the alcoholic husband just because he is the stronger member of the marriage? That brings up a legitimate question. If a dominated wife is married to an alcoholic husband and she obtains a divorce against his will, is she still dominated? In the example I gave in the previous paragraph, she could be dominated if she lets herself be. And some are, even after they get divorced and separated, as I have indicated. But if she has the ego strength to get a divorce, remarry, and make a whole new life for herself, the argument does not seem to hold up that she is the abused one. If the divorce is obtained against her husband's wishes and she wins, she was obviously in charge of events at the end. She lost many battles, but won the decisive one, and the war. This is what many martyred wives of alcoholic husbands end up doing. That's why I am addressing them.

If your husband is and has been the controlling partner of the marriage and he is now an alcoholic, he is no longer capable of remaining the boss. This may be compared to a situation in which a gunman has been holding a group of people under his control with a six-shooter. If it is known that he has only six bullets and they have all been fired, he is holding people with an empty gun. Any man who has become addicted to alcohol has shot his last bullet as far as his ability to run the marriage is concerned, once you know it. You must, of course, discover this fact before it is useful to you. We must also take into account that if you have had ten or twenty years of taking orders, you cannot be easily taught how to take over the marriage. But you can, just enough to save him.

Not all wives have been told this. In the marriages of most alcoholics where the husband has been the stronger figure, his real power begins to slip, and the wife slowly but surely begins to assume the reins as his addiction grows and his ability to rule shrinks. Even though in some cases the appearances of power and influence remain intact, the real decision-making role is assumed by the wife. But that's a different situation from the one I will deal with now.

If you are a wife who thinks you cannot get your way with your alcoholic husband, you must understand your alcoholic's vital needs. He needs your love and sympathy between drunks and between drinks. Deep within himself he knows—in a way he may take months or years or a lifetime to admit—that he is hooked, *he is addicted*. He thinks he "knows" he cannot get along without alcohol and he knows that when he is in the full clutches of alcohol he cannot take care of himself. It is because of this awful knowledge—that he cannot get along *with* alcohol and that he cannot get along *without* it—that causes him to work so hard and so desperately to maintain the status quo, not to change anything in his life. He sees *any* change as threatening to his continued need for alcohol, and since most plans for help really involve his giving up his lifesaving elixir, he fights it with all his might. But the beautiful truth, the saving grace of the whole situation, is that he needs the love and understanding of a real human being—and all the other bonuses that go with being a married man and father—more than he needs the alcohol. This is why presenting a *dependable, attainable, tangible alternative* is going to succeed.

Let us assume that you have returned from your first meeting. You may be sure he is very aware of where you have been even though he may have acted as if he had forgotten all about it. He was probably as much aware of the time and your leaving as you were. Most alcoholic husbands no matter how clever they seem to be are going to let slip that they are aware of the meeting. They may even ask questions about it. First, let's consider how to handle the questions.

Question: "Well, what happened at the meeting?" (This is for the brief spoken type, the kind who doesn't want to use a lot of words since he can depend on his wife to do plenty of filling in and talking. But you're going to surprise him a little.)

Answer: "Well, it was mostly talking." ("What," thinks the husband, "no sermon? No long talk about how thrilled she was and how much she wishes I had been there?")

Question: "Well, for the love of Pete, what did they talk about?" (You will note that he still isn't going to bring up the ugly topic—drinking, alcohol, alcoholism—and all those other unpleasant subjects.)

Answer: "I guess they talked about everything." (Period. You are not going to take the bait. You are not going to try to persuade him to go. You are not going to try to sell him on the idea. You are going to leave him dangling. You are going to make him curious, if it's possible. You are not going to satisfy his curiosity. You are going to keep your answers *brief* and *truthful.*)

Question: "Damn it, Marge. What did they talk about? I'll bet I know. I'll bet they talked about alcoholics and people like me. I'll bet that was it, wasn't it? Why don't you tell me? Hell, you're just wasting your time anyway, but it sure isn't going to help if you don't tell me about it, now is it?"

Hey! Now he's beginning to take the bait himself. Now he's beginning to let it slip that he really wants to know. And what should you do? Stay in the same theme as before. *Do not relent.* Do not satisfy his need to know. Of course, his curiosity is not going to be overpowering now anyway.

Answer: "Well, they did talk about alcoholism." (Period. Again you do not need to say anymore. The less you say, the better your long-term chances of getting him there. Make him curious. Make him beg. But don't try to answer.)

Another good reason for not answering the questions of any alcoholic when you have been to an alcoholism meeting of any kind is that you are not going to be able to do it justice. An alcoholic's wife has too many prejudices and too many emotional involvements to be able to grasp the meaning of things she may have been hearing for the first time. You probably could not possibly repeat everything an alcoholism counselor told you and do it right. The message you received from him was meant for you the moment it was being spoken and in reply to the mood and attitude being expressed at that moment. Such one-to-one communications are delicate and fragile things and cannot easily be transported across town, digested, and then retold in the same way as the first time—even if you could recall all the words. And for the same reason you could not repeat what you heard at an AA meeting or at a meeting of Al-Anon. In addition to that, the things said at AA sessions or Al-Anon meetings are not supposed to be repeated. It is a sacred tradition that what alcoholics and their close kin or spouses say at meetings is supposed to "stay there." The best advice for you then is not to try to explain these encounters or experiences to your alcoholic. Invariably you will fail to tell it correctly. You will also be more likely to give in to the temptation of trying to persuade your alcoholic husband to start going by showing too much enthusiasm or anxiety about the event and his reactions. And this, translated into words, is going to be interpreted by him into unfavorable and unpleasant language. He is going to associate it with other times and situations in which you did try to convince him to go to an AA meeting or to a minister, psychiatrist, or a counselor. So he is going to reject it before you get through.

Once more, the rule is: Don't try to persuade him to go to the meeting. And don't try to explain what happened at the meeting because it is going to sound like you are trying to persuade him. You might tell yourself to "take the Fifth Amendment." Don't answer his questions in detail because anything you say is going to tend to incriminate you—meaning, incriminate you in trying to convince him he's got to do some of these things. Later you may have to do that. But don't jump the gun now. Remember, if he is a chronic alcoholic, even if he has been the master, the ruler of the roost, you now know the truth. He has run out of bullets. You are going to be able to get something happening that you could not have done before. You are going to take over just to the extent necessary to save his life, to save your marriage, and to save him from the certain death or insanity by alcoholism.

But suppose upon returning from your meeting your sly, old alcoholic husband is not around. Suppose he's not even at home or in his den or asleep. What then? The answer to this is short. Just make sure that you register in his mind that you went to the meeting. Make sure he knows you went. Make sure he understands that just because he did not go and wanted to ignore the event altogether that *you* have not ignored it, *you* have not decided again to do nothing. This time you did something. This time something happened. And you want to be certain that you get the full psychological benefit from it. So you want to make certain to register, to make a recording of the fact on his mental tape recorder, so he will be playing it back to himself.

This isn't to back down on the proposition of no obvious selling or persuading. But you do want him to be aware of your going to the meeting, and you want to be sure he isn't allowed to forget about it. So, upon returning from a meeting (and you are going for his good in the final analysis), the one straightforward and honest approach you can give him is to record the fact that you went.

My advice usually is to make the second report announcement with the same care as you made the first announcement. When he is sober and alert and in a good frame of mind you say something just to record the fact that you did get there. And you indicate you liked it by saying you are going back. You might say something like this:

"By the way, I went to see that counselor yesterday, and I am going again to see him Tuesday morning if you want to go."

That's all you say at this point. It is likely that he's going to remind you that his first reaction had been very negative, that he was not going, and would never go. You will not allow this to discourage you at all. Yes, I know you heard him the first time, but you must take all his reactions with a grain of salt and with a great deal of intelligent analysis and hope.

You are not going to be dissuaded from continuing your plan. You are going right ahead. And you are going to take his strong negative responses, no matter how strong and final they may sound, and disregard them.

When you get a strong negative reaction from him you are going to say to yourself these truthful and soothing words:

"Remember, he is an alcoholic. All he hears is 'stop drinking,' which is very frightening to him. Eventually, he is going to accept because deep down within him he does want help because he needs it!" Repeat this to yourself as often as you need to.

So, you are going to repeat your casual invitation upon returning from the meeting: "I went to the counselor yesterday, and I am going back Tuesday morning, *if you want to go.*"

Answer: "Damn it all, Marge. I told you I wasn't going. I told you I never intended to go to one of those people. I am not an alcoholic. I don't need help. I'll stop drinking whenever I decide I need to. So forget it."

No matter how negative the words, remember the anger means it is important to him. The more vehemence he expresses, the more anger he lets out, the more the fact that you are doing something that is disturbing him. If he were not disturbed, he would simply reply no he wasn't going, and let it go. If he gives that kind of a calm answer, you have got a bigger problem than if he gets angry. As I have said before, if he is able to be cool and collected about it, he feels comfortably able to handle you, and he probably can. So beware, don't let it encourage you, but rather, let it make you even more determined to pursue the course right to the end.

Once you get your second announcement about having been to the meeting stated, do just as you did after the first announcement if his response has been negative: *Drop the subject*. Don't try to sell or persuade. Don't cry and don't nag. Drop the subject and go on to something else, some other subject, or some other task.

But do get it said. Don't let the meeting get by without having had your money's worth. This means telling him you did it. Getting that registered with him at this time is about all you can do for him. But it is a lot. It is very important.

In spite of the lack of nagging and crying, in spite of the fact that you no longer talk about his drinking, and even in spite of the fact that you are not trying to get rid of his supply of alcohol—and don't complain when he goes to buy more—he knows what is going on. He knows that this doesn't mean you want him to drink or that you don't care that he is drinking himself drunk every night or every weekend as he has done in the past. He may from time to time wonder out loud if you have changed your basic attitude, that is, of being opposed to his drinking. Since you cannot honestly say that you have, you will have to be careful how to handle that too. It might go like this:

Question: "Hey, I notice you've stopped fussing so much—I notice you don't raise Cain when I go to get a drink. What does that mean? Is it really okay with you now for me to have a little drink sometimes?"

Beware. He thinks he's going to get the upper hand again, and he may if you don't handle this right. Also, beware lest you get into your preaching attitude again.

Answer: "I'm just trying to control *myself* and what *I* do, Jim. *I* can't control what you do."

This answer should stop him in his tracks. You haven't approved of his drinking and you haven't condemned it. You have talked about controlling *yourself*. That's what you can do something about. When you start getting angry and making demands on him, you are going to lose some control of yourself and say things you wish later you had left unsaid. But you haven't done that. You have given him an honest answer. Let's examine what it means to him, your active alcoholic:

He thinks to himself: H'mmm. Control *herself*? Well, I get it. She's not really talking about controlling *herself*. She really means controlling *me*. She really means I ought to control myself. Ha! She's telling me to control myself. She's telling me to quit!

He says, aloud: "Yeah, I get it. You're really telling me I ought to control myself and stop myself from drinking. Well, I'll stop when I'm ready, woman!"

Or, he might end his statement with:

"And stop telling me to control myself. Won't you ever leave me alone?"

So he's trying to say that you are interfering in his life again and lead you into another argument. What your alcoholic really wants is to make you get him angry so he can drink more and get drunk because of your "lack of understanding" for him. But you didn't really do that. So you repeat the statement. That's all you do!

"Jim, I said I was just trying to control myself and what I do. As I said, I *really* cannot control what *you* do."

So far the plan consists of registering the meetings, interviews, or counseling sessions with him *before* each one of them and *after* each one. Each time the alcoholic hears the report I-went-to-a-meeting, it burns itself into his psyche as if with a branding iron.

Every time you tell him, do it with deftness and with very tender care. It should not be easily interpreted by him as "why-in-the-hell-aren't-you-going-too?" If that's the way you feel about it, push that from your mind. The *feeling* that you should be conveying to him is that you are enjoying these meetings, you are changing some of your attitudes, maybe it is fun, and there is hope. It is likely that you are beginning to enjoy them. I hope you are beginning to make some changes in your attitudes and you do feel some hope.

Be certain that you don't share that hope or feeling with him with words. Once again he is likely to misinterpret and think it's the same old argument you have made in the past. He is going to think it is the same old failure playing again, the same old tired and tiresome game of old. So don't use words. Just express your hope and added cheer (if it is really there) in your smile and in being more relaxed. But don't ask him to go with you with any more words than you did the first time. Just make certain he knows the invitation is always there and that he is free and welcome to come. Just don't say it with those words. Say it each time as if it were the first, as if you really expect him to accept.

It can be expected that after about two or three meetings—each announced before they occur and each reported briefly after they occur—that he knows the invitation—"if you want to go" or "don't you want to come?"—is always there. You may not have to add the actual invitational words anymore. After two or three announcements, "Well, I went to Bill Jones the counselor this morning and I'm going again Friday at 9 o'clock." Or, "I went to the AA meeting [or the Al-Anon meeting] last night and I'm going again Wednesday." He'll know he's welcome to come. He'll know that's why you mention the time. He'll know that is why you mention it at all. Why else would you be mentioning that you are going back except to let him know that he's still welcome and that you haven't stopped expecting him to accept and come with you. If it's Al-Anon, of course, the implication is for him to go to AA while you are at Al-Anon. Usually meetings are held simultaneously and at the same place.

You must always keep up the "and I am going again" part of the announcement. This tells him something clearly. That is that you are getting something out of it, that you like it, that you really want him to know you like it, and that you still understand (as you do at this point deep down) that he would really like to go even though he has never so much as smiled when you said it.

Suppose he has been fighting it with extra anger and vehemence. Suppose that he interrupts you each time you begin to utter the words "I've been to a meeting and I am going back Tuesday." What then?

First, you should take this as *encouraging*. The words and their meaning are getting to him deep down where it hurts and where it may just turn the trick. If they weren't, he would not react adversely to them. He would not get excited if he found it easy to fluff them off. He would not get angry over something that didn't matter to him. Remember, you haven't preached and scolded and really fought him for a long time at this point. Maybe it has been several weeks since you changed from the nagging, frightened wife of old into a smart, knowledgeable planner using guided intervention techniques. So why should he be getting angry just because you say you have been to a meeting and are going again unless it really does affect him? The truth is it is causing him great concern. Probably he feels he is going to be forced to respond to you and be forced to face his problem. It is a most frightening prospect for any alcoholic, although it is what must come to pass if you are to achieve success.

But being encouraged about his anger may not help you to accept his attacks on you. *Words can* hurt, especially from a loved one and especially when you are trying to walk in new and strange places. So what do you do? How can you handle these hostile attacks?

The way to handle them is to remember the original rule for handling all negative responses to all the announcements. Be brief. Be truthful. Some suggested responses to his anger over the frequent repeated announcements about meetings might be one of these:

Answer A: "Okay, Jim, I'm sorry I upset you."

Isn't that backing down? Is that what I really mean? Is that honest? No, you won't be backing down. You told him about the meeting just to get it to register. His anger was a real it-has-registered signal. You've done your job. You do not need to add to it. So you are sorry. You are sorry it got him upset. You aren't sorry you said it, though, because you are going to say it again *before* the next meeting and *after* the next meeting and you are going to keep that up. You are only sorry it upset him.

Answer B: "I just wanted you to know where I've been"—or "where I'm going to be."

That is truthful and brief. Not honest you say? Well, you want him to know where you have been *not* for your safety or in case he wants to find you but so he will *know you are doing something* about the problem. There's no need to explain the full meaning.

Answer C: Complete calm silence. By your not saying anything you cut the argument down to size. No response is a strong response. It says to him that you are not going to fight, that you are not taking back what you said, but that you also are not trying to hit him over the head with it. You got your message across. That is all you wanted. So you don't need to add anything to it, and you don't.

You can use one of these three alternative responses every time. One of the three will almost always do the trick. After all, what he is responding to with such deep feeling is a short uncontroversial statement of fact. You have been to a meeting or you are going to a meeting. What's the excitement about? Can't he even take that much? The answer is that he doesn't have a choice. He will take it.

Suppose he handles it another way. Suppose he starts to cut you off before you are even through with your statement:

"Well, I went to a meeting with Bill Jones. . . ."

He: "Yeah, I know and you're going to another one Tuesday. So what?"

You: "Well, as a matter of fact, I am going Tuesday." Or, "As a matter of fact our next meeting is Wednesday."

The point is to *register* the fact. That gets the job done.

It once again burns into his brain that you are continuing to do something, that something is going on, that something new and different is beginning to happen.

Once again, that is *all* you do. Keep it up. Don't relent. Don't lose an opportunity to report that you have been to a meeting and never fail to report that you are going to a meeting. Do not ever report either fact more than once. Once is enough. Once *after* each meeting and once *before* each meeting. But one of the important reasons for going is to be able to report it. Your going to the meeting and his knowledge of this activity is worth more than a thousand angry words.

5

If He Stops Drinking and Bargains

Your alcoholic may respond to guided intervention techniques in one of several nonverbal ways. He may slow up noticeably on his drinking. He may increase it noticeably, too. Or, third, he may begin some of the manipulations he has used in the past just to get you to stop doing what you are doing. Do not be led astray.

The hardest response of all for you to handle will be that he stops drinking. This is the alcoholic's ultimate manipulation, the master stroke. Do not jump to conclusions about the future or about his alcoholism. Every alcoholic can stop at some point or another for a while. Some can stop for a few days, some for a few weeks, and some for many months. But practically none can stop permanently without going through some kind of treatment, without some kind of knowledgeable help. So do not be led astray.

Almost always when your alcoholic stops or slows down his drinking he will ask a favor of you. He may tell you that he will stop or slow down on the condition that you stop going to those "silly" consultations or "silly" group therapy meetings or "stupid" Al-Anon or AA meetings. Do not bargain. Under no circumstances should you treat his not drinking or, even less, treat his slowing down of drinking as something to bargain about. The only time he is going to stop drinking effectively is when he realizes that he, himself, is the one being hurt, not you or someone else. If he tries to bargain with you that way respond like this:

"Jim, if you want to stop or slow down your drinking, that's fine. But I'm not making any bargain about what I do myself. *I* need these sessions myself. For me. And I'm going to keep going."

This will be hard for him to handle. He will likely respond with something like the following:

"You mean you are going to keep up this silly business even if I quit drinking? I thought that was why you were going. I still think that's it. So I am going to quit drinking. If you are really honest and fair about it, you'll stop these time-consuming meetings, or wasting our money by seeing this counselor."

Don't take the bait. Once again you must hold your ground. Tell him once again that if he wants to stop drinking or anything else he wants to do it is all right with you. Don't show enthusiasm for it because he knows—and you should know by now—that it is not going to last. But you are going to keep on doing what you have been doing because *you* need help. *You* are the one going to the meetings for help.

If he gets drunk after you refuse to stop going, take that as encouragement. This is his last desperate test of your determination. Handle it the best way you can but do not be blackmailed by it. Remember, the soothing, truthful words of chapter 4 and repeat them to yourself.

But suppose, despite everything you do, he does stop drinking and keeps on nagging you about your activities. What then? Doesn't this really prove he is not an alcoholic? Doesn't this prove he was right when he told you he could quit whenever he decided to? Hasn't this already accomplished the job of guided intervention? Why is it necessary, as he continues asking, to keep on going to these sessions with a counselor or to these Al-Anon meetings or to open AA meetings? When an alcoholic stops drinking permanently it is usually the result of help he accepts under pressure. The alcoholic who *stops drinking* because of pressure without treatment, strange as it may sound, is actually putting the carriage before the horse. He is stopping because he wants to feel free to start again when he is ready! He is stopping because he doesn't want to face the truth of his predicament. He is playing a game. He is trying to keep full control of the situation in which he decides *when* he can drink and *when* he won't drink. He can abstain as long as he knows the decision to drink again is still open, undisturbed, and that no more antidrinking arguments have been thrown in to muddy the water.

You can recognize this game and distinguish it from the true desire not to drink, the real beginning of permanent sobriety, by looking for certain signals that are likely to be present when he stops on his own terms. These are the signals:

1. He will be telling you that he is stopping not because he is an "alcoholic" but just to prove to you that he is *not* an alcoholic.

2. He will not be stopping permanently, he will tell you himself, but only for "a long time" or another impressive period. He may or may not set himself a goal. If he does set a goal, you can be certain he is going to drink again at the expiration of the self-imposed abstinence.

3. He will refuse all help. This will be a vital part of his not drinking. He won't go to AA. He won't go to a counselor. He won't visit with AA people. He will avoid mention of alcoholism. This, he will tell you, will all be part of the proof that he is not really an alcoholic. Since he isn't, he will argue, he certainly won't need any "crutches" to stop drinking.

4. More than likely he will not get rid of the alcoholic beverages around the house.

5. More than likely he will make many demands on you since (he will rationalize) he is doing it all for you and therefore you will owe him something in return.

6. He will likely threaten you, subtly or directly, with the possibility of drinking again when he gets irritated with you or wants something from you.

The reason these signals indicate the opposite of what he is telling you is that the only valid and finally effective reason for anyone to quit drinking after alcohol has become so important in his life is to discover that it is *hurting* him. All things being equal, we all tend to do what will benefit us, ourselves. We are unable to keep ourselves from doing something just because we are told it helps someone else. If your alcoholic tries to stop drinking only because you want him to, it is inevitable that eventually he is going to drink again noting—quite reasonably to himself— that it cannot hurt you if you don't know about it.

The reason your alcoholic does not claim he is quitting forever is that the thought of that, as I have previously observed, is more than he can accept. But as long as he knows he will be able to drink again sometime ("after I've proved I'm not an alcoholic"), he can endure the pain of abstinence because it is temporary.

He refuses all help, not because he doesn't feel that he needs it, but because to him "help" means only one thing: permanent abstinence.

He is unlikely to get rid of the alcohol around the house so that he can feel the security of knowing it is there for an "emergency." Of course, he may not tell you that, but it is the reason.

He will make demands on you because he will resent the fact that you, in his mind, have put him in this most uncomfortable position of not being able to drink. Yes, he's going to blame you even though he claims it is his own doing. You will be blamed for the discomfort and the pain. He will take credit for being strong enough to do it.

He will threaten you from time to time with the suggestion that he is going to drink not because he wants to frighten you or hurt you but because he will be wanting to drink so badly.

But suppose your alcoholic stops drinking for six months, six long months. Isn't that real evidence of his not being an alcoholic?

No, it is not.

What about a whole year? That should be proof, shouldn't it, especially if he has never done it before.

The answer is still no. Not drinking for a year is not a sign of nonalcoholism. It is a sign of strength to control. It is also a sign of a desperate and unhappy man who needs to feel he can keep drinking the rest of his life even more than he may feel he needs to drink at the moment.

Wait a minute! I can hear you saying. You mean to tell me an alcoholic can stop drinking for a whole year—or that a person who can stop drinking for a whole year hasn't proved he is not an alcoholic?

Yes, that's what I am saying. If the six signals of game playing are present, it is a certain sign that his alcoholism is merely being controlled. After all, couldn't you give up a year of living with your most beloved person if it meant that you would be able to live with him contentedly the rest of your life? That's the way it appears to the alcoholic. Alcohol is his life, his hope, his surcease from all problems, his greatest love. Yes, he'll do without it for six months or a year (if he is a disciplined kind of person) just to prove his point. But, more important, he will do it so he can drink without this continuing interference the rest of his life. After he has stopped for a year or six months, he has got the perfect alibi: I quit for a year, didn't I? So how could I be an alcoholic?

The only way we can be sure that alcoholism is being conquered is to have at least two years of continuous sobriety together with mature therapeutic activity the whole while. If a long period of sobriety by itself were enough, all the alcoholics who were locked up in hospitals or penitentiaries where they were forcibly denied access to liquor would leave "cured." But the record shows that they do not. The typical alcoholic kept away from his booze for a long period of time goes right back to it as soon as it becomes available again.

Again, I say. If your problem drinker stops drinking for a long period of time, watch for those six game signals. I think you will find them present almost every time.

It may be hard to accept, but even if a person who had been suspected of alcoholism stopped drinking for two whole years, it would not disprove his having crossed the line into alcoholism earlier. I have known of many alcoholics who have stopped for even longer than two years—but without obtaining proper help and without accepting their condition—only to return to their old drinking patterns every single time.

The alcoholic may stop drinking and not give you the *game* signals. He may make some demonstration of accepting the fact that he had a problem. He may not object to your continuing your going to counseling, AA, or Al-Anon. Then there may be reason for hope.

But to be certain you should put these minimum conditions on the change of events: 1) That he not stop you (the nonalcoholic) from doing whatever you choose to do; 2) That some real sign of a change of life-style or attitude really takes place in his life, such as a genuine religious experience or a serious lasting interest in some other emotional resource; 3) You should also look for some euphemism for his alcoholism that he can accept and live with in explaining himself and his change; 4) You should not begin to relax until after at least three years of total abstinence. Above all, do not stop what *you* are doing.

Of course, all these foregoing conditions are wiped out if he should start going to AA or to some other alcoholism therapy. I would completely rule out his trying to substitute a psychiatrist, marriage counselor, minister, or other professional person who did not *specialize* in alcoholism. If he did that, it would be a further sign of manipulation on his part, a further sign that he was playing a game.

In conclusion, the rule for handling a husband who stopped drinking would be this: Accept his change of behavior, day to day, but do not *under any circumstances* give up your efforts. From my experience I think you will find almost every time that his abstaining is going to be short-lived. More than likely, your problem is going to get back to the original proposition. So remember: no nagging, no fussing, no lecturing, no persuading. You continue going to the meetings and continue the regular invitations. Follow-ups will come later.

One final and perhaps unnecessary word. If your alcoholic uses moderating his drinking as a means of trying to show you he is "not an alcoholic," treat him and his behavior in the same way as you would total abstinence. The chances are that he will go back to getting drunk again even sooner than when he abstained completely. But he may be able to keep it up for an impressive time. Do not be misled and do not under any circumstances bargain or be manipulated out of your program. If he does begin to impress you, the chances are that he is secretly drinking more than you are being allowed to see and that he is concentrating on showing it less. If the almost impossible should happen and he moderates his drinking and never gets drunk or even slightly high over a long period of time, you may not have an alcoholic on your hands. But, before you decide this, I would want to see the drinking moderated for longer than one year. Only then could you conceivably reach such a happy conclusion. But, if your husband were not an alcoholic, the chances are he would not have objected to your activities in the first place. So, the rule still is: Don't be talked out of pursuing help for yourself and your problem.

6

Are You Certain You Want Him to Recover?

Some years ago I was visiting the Metropolitan Workhouse in my city when I spotted one of my former Samaritan Center clients sweeping the floor of the dining room. He wore the distinctive white suit of the prisoners. I knew him for a bright and articulate homeless alcoholic for whom I had once entertained fond hope. In conversation he seemed unlike my conception of a skid row bum. The thought flashed through my mind that I might try once again to bring about a change in him at Samaritan and confirm my hopes for him.

"Hi, Jimmy," I said. And after a few more ritual exchanges I broached the subject. "Why don't you give up all this," I said, waving at the bars and the cold steel tables and the guards in the place, "and come back to the Samaritan House [that's what we called it then] where you belong?"

Jimmy smiled his pleasant smile, pleased by the recognition and affection that I was expressing, leaned against his broom and said, philosophically, "You know, Roque, this isn't really so bad. It *really* isn't."

The truth was out. Jimmy, who might have been a successful newspaperman, radio announcer, salesman, or who knows what, was growing satisfied with his lot in life. He was beginning to adjust. He knew how to respond to squad car policemen when they drove up beside him and ordered him in. He knew how to face judges with little pain or embarrassment. He knew the worst that could happen to him after or during a drunk, and he knew and relished the best that did happen to him. His best was to be locked up in the workhouse and to have dining-room duty instead of the rock pile or hard labor. What to me was degrading and sad, abhorrent and disgraceful, was to Jimmy "really not so bad."

I could also conclude that he found it more comfortable than facing the grind of daily confrontation with his alcoholism problem at the Samaritan Center. It wasn't that Jimmy did not like us at the center. I felt he did. Our therapy was not hard to endure. But it involved taking the whole program. It involved admitting his alcoholism, going through the long-term pain of abstinence. It further involved trying to get proper medical attention for his physical complaints, trying to win back acceptance from his long-estranged wife and daughter. This was painful to face because there was little reason to expect success. Jimmy had tried and failed several times. He would have to endure all these pains and discomforts, long waits, and uncertain promises of tangible rewards without any relief from his staunchest and most reliable friend, his alcohol.

I have seen Jimmy two or three times since. When I see him I cry a little inside. He is a pathetic figure. He is crippled, walking with a slight limp. He is also small and thin. He is usually drunk and on the way back to jail (very soon he will be accosted by his friends, the police) or just shortly out of jail, having just served another of his installments on a life term. But I cannot invest the time to try to persuade Jimmy one more time to try to change his whole life through our agency. The truth is, bitter as it may be to accept, that Jimmy is resigned to his fate. He will accept his brief rewards in a warm workhouse dining room and moderately good food, and his carefree moments of downing some cheap wine with his derelict friends for a few hours or a few days and then pay the price. The price is the insults of the sometimes sadistic, sometimes unfeeling representatives of the establishment in uniforms or on a bench in a court of uncertain justice. The price includes the pain of withdrawal from alcohol with its accompanying nightmares of horror-filling sights and sounds, the pain of occasional unattended illness, the pain of being mugged, rolled, or beaten by stronger and younger derelict alcoholics. But Jimmy's mind has been conditioned not to see further ahead than the next drink or the next warm meal. So he doesn't accept our help and he won't. Not for now. And there is at present no one outside the law with the legal authority to change the situation.

I have had to learn how to accept the Jimmys whom I have met, experience some success with, and then lose touch with them. I have accepted Jimmy's decision but I despise it and I have not locked the door. I say the prayer of Reinhold Niebuhr:

"God, grant me the serenity to accept the things I cannot change, courage to change the things I can, and wisdom to know the difference." And I add the words attributed to Admiral Chester Nimitz:

"But God, grant me the courage not to give up on what I think is right even though I think it is hopeless."

Jimmy and many thousands like him might be helped with involuntary confinement in an institution geared to meeting his special needs and structured to return his full freedoms to him by degrees over a period of many months. But that is another story.

I have delayed my point in this chapter with the story of Jimmy, my derelict alcoholic friend, because Jimmy is so much like the *wives* of many alcoholics I have known. Not the *alcoholics,* but their wives. If I were to address the title of this chapter to the Jimmys, it would read "Are You Certain You Want to Recover?" No doubt the Jimmys would say,

"Are you crazy? Sure, I want to recover; just tell me what to do." Which is what you, the wife of an alcoholic reading this, are saying to yourself: "Are you serious? Certainly, I want him to stop drinking and change his life and recover. Just tell me what to do." It may offend you and it may be an odious comparison but I must make it. I am sure the same reply in the same spirit would come from many prostitutes when questioned by a social worker. "The only reason I do this kind of work is that I don't know any other. I need the income to keep my child in clothes and in a good school." Then the prostitute would add: "But if you can show me a way to make a good living and help me to get that kind of work, I'll give up this life." How many prostitutes are leaving the profession as a result of outside intervention? Why aren't they leaving? I think the reason is similar to Jimmy's—and to the many wives of alcoholics I have known. They find the pain and discomfort of a change of life intolerable after having adjusted themselves to the one they are in. This is true even though their present life involves pain and humiliation at the hands of the police and others for the Jimmys. As for wives of alcoholics, their lives involve problems of making a living as the head of the house or being humiliated and embarrassed by the unpredictable conduct of their alcoholic. But they have adjusted to it.

In plain English: The biggest obstacle I have met in trying to reach alcoholics with guided intervention hasn't been alcoholics. It has been nonalcoholic mates. When I have succeeded in keeping the wife of an alcoholic involved in a program, I have always eventually reached the alcoholic. The trouble is I have not always been able to keep the nonalcoholics involved long enough to succeed. The reason? There can only be one answer: The wife has found it easier or more comfortable to live with the problem than to struggle for the solution.

In the American dream family the wife is viewed as a home manager of children and food, house and car. She runs the home; her husband runs the office and brings home the money with which the expenses are paid. The marriage is fifty-fifty. The husband-father cuts the lawn, tends to the mechanical problems of the home and cars, and shares in disciplining the children and in the family relationship with relatives and social groups and individuals. In this dream family the husband and wife love one another and have no need for extramarital adventures. They share each other's joys and sorrows as they share the love each has for the other. They teach their children to do the same and to expect the same in the children's marriages.

But the American ideal family is frequently too easy to fake and too shocking to face when it turns out phony. This is particularly and peculiarly true of alcoholic marriages. It becomes traumatic to admit failure. It becomes almost an irreversible situation to enjoy and promote social drinking of alcoholic beverages one day and then a little later to say out loud that the same beverages are home-destroyers and unacceptable. Even when that occurs and it does occur in most alcoholic marriages—how can the drinker himself be declared sick? Or condemned? One time he is sociable and fun, a delight in conversation. Next time he is an embarrassment and an unpredictable maniac. Or, take the alcoholic person apart from his drinking. He is a hardworking and dependable breadwinner, a leading figure in his profession. He may be a leading attorney or a vice-president in charge of sales. He may be a leading physician to whom thousands of trusting patients know they can safely turn for help. How can we turn "against" *him* to do things he insists he does not need.

The wife of an alcoholic is often confronted with a contradiction. Her husband loves her, cares for her and the children and the home 95 percent of the time. He is admired and respected and liked. When another friend's husband becomes addicted to alcohol himself, the friend comes to her husband! How could this same man be a victim of alcoholism? Could anything be more difficult to accept?

"He is a good man. He is reliable. He is so admired by everyone who knows him. He is respected. He is a hard worker. He would die if he knew I was here seeing you! He really does love me and the children." These are the phrases I have been hearing repeatedly for years. They have been used to describe chronic alcoholics. They have been used to describe alcoholics who in drunken moments have beaten and maimed their wives and children. They have described alcoholics who have uttered four-letter gutter language in the most public places. They have described alcoholics who have had not one but three and four arrests for drunken driving. They have described alcoholics who haven't worked for years or whose game playing at working has produced but a token income for their family's needs.

The problem is that wives of alcoholics contract the twin malady of co-alcoholism. They are co-alcoholics when they begin to share the system of delusions, the make-believe world of their alcoholics. They are co-alcoholics when they begin to adjust to the drunken behavior of their alcoholic, to his need for alcohol above everything else. They are co-alcoholics when they begin to feel satisfied if he drinks himself into a stupor and doesn't *bother* anyone else. They are co-alcoholics when they can live day in and day out with this unreliable and unpredictable kind of person just because they can recall that he was not always like that. Finally, it has become incurable co-alcoholism if the co-alcoholic cannot endure sharing the alcoholic's pain and its ramifications while he is abstaining. It is the most tragic kind of chronic co-alcoholism when the co-alcoholic cannot endure to have the alcoholic sober!

Look deep inside yourself. Are you certain you want him to recover? Will you be able to stand a sober husband in the place of the quiet unobtrusive one you have been having all these months or years? Will you be able to tolerate the nagging that he may direct at you when you insist on doing the things you do to try to help him? It is going to be one of the hardest things you have undertaken in your life. You may have to give it more thought than you imagined before trying. You may need to discuss it in depth with your counselor, AA friend, or fellow Al-Anon member. You may need to postpone taking action for a while. Maybe you need to wait a few weeks or even months until you have fully prepared yourself for the ordeal.

I do not want to discourage you. Neither do I want to accept but one answer to this question. I believe every woman married to an alcoholic who reads this book can find the answer if she will work at it. I am trying to meet and resolve the problems you will have in working at it.

First, your beloved alcoholic husband may appeal to your "common sense" or "intelligence" or "love and understanding" of him. Whatever he calls it, it will be a manipulation, an attempt to make you do his will and not yours. He may ridicule AA if you go. He may ridicule the counselor or the Al-Anon member you befriend. He will remind you of how well he held his liquor in years past. He will remind you of how he has overcome other problems in the past with only your help. Without "outsiders." He will compare your going out for help with unanalogous incidents, with cases of friends that will not be the same. He will do everything in his power to distract you from pursuing your goal. When that fails, he will bring even more pressure. You may be able to win the first round of these pressures because you will recognize them for the repetitions of past failures that they are. But can you persist?

After guided intervention begins to take hold and your husband starts going to meetings or doing whatever else was in your plan, your life at home is going to be different. The changes are not going to be subtle. Each night, for example, instead of having an indifferent husband who may or may not eat supper, you may find a hungry, complaining, and active man who isn't satisfied with the menu. The small portions of casserole and economy dishes that you may have had to learn to eat over the years of his heavy drinking are no longer something of indifference to him. He now sits down with you and tries to eat. He must make up for the energy he had been getting from his alcohol calories. The change is abrupt and painful.

Your indifferent sex life over the years now is changing. Your nondrinking husband suddenly wants to make love to you. Maybe you have long ago lost all interest in sex. Maybe you have thought that women your age and men his age just did not do these things anymore. Now he is alive and wanting to change that. These are some of the changes and adjustments that may prove hard to accept.

In my counseling I have been hearing certain phrases repeated many times. One classic is: "There isn't anything I would not do to help him get over this drinking problem!" This sounds reasonable and sincere. But when put to the test, many wives quit in the face of the simplest kind of task. On occasion the truth will come out despite the intentions of the speaker. I recall one wife who had been coming to me and whose alcoholic husband was staying sober and attending group therapy with her. She was complaining to me in a private session of the problems she was having with him. None were related to drinking. They were emotional problems, related to what he said and did getting home from work, sober and talkative, trying to live a normal life. But she was working, too. She was under pressure both at work and at home. While telling me, she blurted out: "I wish it were like it used to be!" I immediately caught the implications of this and called it to her attention. "In other words, you are saying, he was easier to handle when he was drinking. Right?"

"Well, I guess so," she admitted. And then, she started backing down and denying that she really meant it.

My best example of this was a woman client who had become an executive earning a five-figure income while her husband became a total business failure in his field. He had become the stay-at-home partner in the marriage. She was the breadwinner. He did no housework. He did no cooking. He just stayed at home. Between drinking his beer and whiskey, he dillydallied with dreams and plans that never materialized. When she came to me, this had been going on for five years. There were no children.

This woman was highly successful in her field, hiring and firing, managing people, keeping profits up and losses down, in a good-size business. But when she went home at night, she became the handmaiden of her alcoholic. She not only bought but also washed his expensive shirts. She cooked his meals even when she was tired and in need of rest. She was the one who went to the store for his alcohol. One might have thought her motivation was sex but it wasn't. As with most alcoholics there was little or no sexual intercourse. He had lost his drive from the booze.

I remember my naïveté when this woman first came to see me. I was shocked and incredulous. Later after meeting the husband and confirming the entire story, I told her I was certain we could reach her alcoholic husband. How much easier for successful intervention, I thought, than the usual case. Here was a case where the concerned person supported a husband, a way of life our culture staunchly disapproves. What I learned helped to inspire this chapter.

This lady came to me for months. She participated in group therapy and seemed to grow in it. Later, I used the intervention technique that I will describe later. But Amy was never able to carry out any of my suggestions. They were too painful. She could not endure the sight of her poor Billy trying to do without his alcohol. Finally, she had to admit it. I turned her over to a psychiatrist friend who a year later told me that she was continuing the charade that was her life. Like Jimmy, who found the workhouse not so bad, I had to accept Amy and Billy's tragedy. But I do not like it. I still want to see it changed.

The truth is that there are many thousands like Amy. There are many Amys in need of treatment just as much for their own deluded lives as there are Jimmys. This has led me to conclude that co-alcoholism is just as much a threat to our nine million or more alcoholics in this country as the alcohol itself. Many times I have had to refer the concerned person to a psychiatrist or to other psychotherapy. And a few times I got clear impressions that the husbands being described to me were more wife-abused than alcohol abusers.

Once a woman paid me my fee and never stopped talking for a full hour during which she told me why there was positively no way to help her alcoholic husband. When the hour was up I cut her off and told her I had to agree. I agreed because I thought that with her compulsive talking I would be helpless to reach him *through* her.

Frequently I receive telephone calls from mothers of alcoholics who do the same thing the compulsive talker wife did, without paying a fee. They simply tell me over and over that there just isn't any way anyone can help their sons. When I try to suggest alternatives, they respond by telling me the many reasons why my suggestion will not work. They always conclude therefore that there would not be any point in making an appointment to see a counselor.

Why do they call in the first place? If they don't want help—and they seem to reject all suggestions—why do they bother to start the conversation by saying they are calling to see if there is anything that can be done? The answer is they get the relief they need by talking out their problem. In psychotherapy it is called ventilating. They talk to someone about their alcoholic for fifteen or thirty minutes. That serves their need for many months. Or, until the son or husband dies in an alcohol-related accident or with cirrhosis or DTs or by his own hand.

For the same reason there will be some who will buy this book, read it, and never do more than talk about it. These people are adjusted to their alcoholic's drinking. From time to time they will ventilate their feelings, read books and pamphlets about alcoholism, and do nothing more. Meanwhile their alcoholics drink themselves to death. These co-alcoholics must go through certain motions from time to time to satisfy outraged friends and relatives who see the horror of the situation. They merely pretend to seek help. But they will not accept it because they cannot endure the discomfort and pain of working with a sober alcoholic or fighting with an alcoholic who is struggling to quit.

If you read this and disagree with the idea that genuine love is shown by guided intervention, consider what love means. The very least it can mean is to want someone to stay alive. Therefore, if you *love him enough* you can *give him up* to *save his life.* Consider the picture if it were some other kind of illness, a highly contagious and incurable disease that you contracted. You would not insist on living with him the rest of his life if that meant he was exposing himself to your disease and would die of it, would you? Consider such a situation. You have a disease that he will get if he continues to live with you. Are you going to insist that he stay with you on the grounds that he cannot live without you? Will you claim there is no other solution for him than to continue this certain-to-be-fatal exposure "*because you love him?*" Who could argue that successfully? Certainly, if it were the other way around—if he had the disease and you did not—your decision would not be the same.

Do not argue that the analogy is false. It is true. The principle in guided intervention is simple: If you love him enough to leave him to save his life, you can carry out the procedure and get him well. You don't have to leave him, necessarily. In my experiences with guided intervention I have seen only one divorce. It occurred on the instigation of the nonalcoholic husband long after the alcoholic wife had stopped drinking. The rest of my experience has been to see marriages survive, even after separations, trials, and hardships. But, even if you had to leave him, if it would save him from alcoholism, wouldn't it be worth it?

It takes courage and determination to persist in guided intervention. It takes the same amount of courage to look at yourself honestly and openly. Forcing the issue with a strong-willed alcoholic man can be a debilitating experience. I do not deny it. It may even be beyond your strength. I don't deny that either. But for the sake of your alcoholic, I am entering a plea that if that is the case—if you do not have the strength to oppose him long enough to achieve success—call it what it is and do not blame something else.

In considering alternative actions finally to get your alcoholic to accept help and to continue in a treatment plan, I will later propose that when all else has failed, you separate from him and finally, if necessary, that you get a legal separation. It is my conviction that to continue to support an active alcoholic in his drinking is to be a partner in a suicide pact. I believe that every time you give an alcoholic love in any form, while he continues to kill himself with alcohol, you are being an accessory to his self-destruction.

I have had co-alcoholic women clients who have continued to live with and accept their alcoholic's drinking behavior on the grounds that they were not strong enough to oppose him. I think that looked at under the cold light of reality any one of these women could have at least had the courage to walk out on her man even if she couldn't do anything else. Staying with him, while all the while complaining, nagging, and then alternately putting up with and rejecting his drinking, comes close to being an unspoken kind of suicide pact. Wives so inclined need psychotherapy as much as their husbands need alcoholism therapy.

A wife and mother came to see me some years ago and described vividly the cruelty and violence of her alcoholic husband. He was also a good wage earner. But once a week he would come home drunk late at night, would attack her, tear off her clothing, and put her out of the house, naked, even in winter. He also engaged in violent and frightening fights with two teen-aged sons. The sons would call him by four-letter words and he would respond in kind. On at least one occasion a son had threatened the father with a loaded gun. This wife's tale of horrors almost knew no end. Finally I interrupted. Why, I asked, why did she continue to live with him? How, in God's name, could she put up with this madness and violence? At first she told me that she frequently asked herself the same question. But finally she admitted the truth. He was a good provider, and she was enjoying the comforts of an air-conditioned home, her own late-model car, fashionable clothes, and a lot of leisure time. She agreed, nevertheless, to enroll in our Azalea Center group therapy and counseling and try to get help for her active alcoholic husband. But as I predicted to her at the time, she discontinued the program after two weeks. It was not difficult to understand. This woman could accept abnormal amounts of irrational behavior by members of her family. She was showing that clearly. She had been accepting it for a long time. The once-weekly drinking behavior of her alcoholic mate was not much more than a common event in her life. Almost any other woman would have yelled wolf much earlier or would have obtained a separation or divorce from such a man. The very fact that she could tell her story almost with gusto was the tip-off. She was not about to upset her fine way of life by trying to force her husband to do anything. To do so might endanger his ability to earn the money he was so happily spending on her. Once again I found myself feeling sympathy for a man who had been described to me as a monster and brute. I knew that unless he found help for himself, he would continue his alcoholic life because he was living with a woman who needed him as a drinking alcoholic.

If you are finding it difficult as you progress through our intervention plan, ask yourself—ask yourself on your knees—if you truly want to make the sacrifice necessary to bring your alcoholic to recovery. If you don't, then have the courage to proceed toward a separation so that he will at least know how hard it is for you to face the situation. In other words, if you cannot go the step-by-step route, go the hard, fast way. It will have the same effect and may save his life in a shorter time. I do not wish to ask you to do what you literally cannot do. But you *can move out* of your home and communicate your true feelings that way. Read on into the chapter on achieving success and apply guided intervention as it best suits you. Remember, the idea is to get your alcoholic into treatment. Not everyone will do it the same way.

7

If You Are the Parent, Child, or Employer

Guided intervention can be applied with varying degrees of success by one or both parents of an alcoholic. It can be applied with more certainty of success by an employer. The child or children of an alcoholic parent find it the most difficult. It will depend in the last case on the cooperation among brothers and sisters involved. All three relationships are taken up in this chapter.

The relationship between a parent and a chronic alcoholic child has many variables. Does the alcoholic still reside with the parents? Is he married, separated, or divorced? Are children involved? His employment or economic status also enters the picture. A parent planning to use guided intervention should first find a counselor by using the same guidelines as suggested for married co-alcoholics. But lest you are saying to yourself that it cannot be done, let me give you the case history that helped me the most. It was my own case with my son.

While living in Florida my son, nicknamed Charlie, then a tender fifteen years old, failed to get home one night until 5:00 a.m. When he did show up he said he had gone to sleep on the beach after drinking half a bottle of vodka that someone had given him. It was the first of many trying and depressing experiences, most of which (it now seems incredible) his mother and I failed to see as alcohol-related. During two years of problems with school and juvenile authorities he amassed a record of three automobile driving arrests, only one officially involving alcohol. It appeared to be another "understandable" boyhood incident. We were like most parents of an adolescent alcoholic, blind to the very end to the true nature of his problem, and, as also occurs many times, we were assured by more than one professional that our son was not "an alcoholic." In addition to the three traffic arrests, and a scuffle in which a telephone booth was damaged, Charlie was expelled from school after showing up drunk at a school dance and insulting the principal. He ran away from home twice, once for two weeks, another with the family car, ending up in a southern Georgia jail. The high school principal failed to tell us of the drunken incident, which did not come to light until years later. At seventeen, after going away to an exclusive boys' prep school, and consultations with a child psychologist who had not been of any help at all, Charlie announced he was ready for marriage. Still in our co-alcoholic delusions we thought marriage to a stable and sweet girl might help him settle down. The girl's parents consented, and the young couple were married in our church.

Charlie and his wife moved to Tennessee where a year later he decided he could solve his continuing and still unidentified "problems" by joining the navy. They had become a family of four when they moved to California. On his first liberty from boot camp Charlie set the pattern of his navy career. (I did not hear of it until years later.) A drunk joy ride in a "borrowed" car earned him his first court-martial in

Hawaii. A second almost identical experience brought a second trial in California with a suspended sentence. The sentence would be invoked only if he had another serious violation. Later, stateside he went AWOL for thirty-three days after he missed his ship. When he made contact with a married sister, I was notified, and I turned him over to the navy shore patrol. Finally, he was discharged with an "undesirable" classification, which he lived with for more than a decade.

Throughout these events—the navy experiences were never told to me until the end—I had never seen him drunk or even mildly high. Once I missed a six-pack of beer from the refrigerator. Charlie admitted drinking it all but I could not tell that he had had any. Most alcoholics build up a tolerance to the chemical others simply cannot imagine. It is one of the vital danger signals that alcoholism is present or just around the corner. Yet, here was Charlie, home after an undesirable discharge from the navy, directly traceable to uncontrolled drinking and a navy psychiatrist's assurance that he was not an alcoholic. I tell this for the benefit of parents or other concerned persons of alcoholics who may be getting the same kind of "expert" advice. The truth is a majority of psychiatrists, psychologists, social workers, and physicians of all specialities (except alcoholism) rarely understand alcoholism, its symptoms, or its remedies *enough to help.* Only now are some medical and other professional schools beginning to introduce alcoholism into their curricula. There are still very few.

My son's alcoholism continued to get progressively worse. After his discharge his suffering wife and children returned from California, and he started working in a manufacturing plant owned by a family friend. On a payday, he got drunk, locked himself in the women's rest room, and was fired. He obtained another job. Then came the first application of some guided intervention. He was jailed for drunk and disorderly conduct and resisting arrest. I went to the jail, indicating my distress and frustration. I bailed him out only after letting him know I would make some demands on him. When he got out I told him to call a member of AA whom I had been urging him to call for several months.

He did and he later became one of the youngest successful members of the fellowship in our town. But only for thirteen months. During his sobriety he neglected his wife for AA, he let bills pile up, and was about to lose his car. Finally, while trying to help a drunken AA friend, he drank some beer himself and got drunk again.

This time he was jailed in a nearby small town after wrecking his car and being chased across an open field by a highway patrolman. He was accompanied by a woman he had picked up in a tavern. This time I let him spend a few days in a small county jail and then, with an attorney to help, paid his fine and took him home. But his wife gave up on him. She returned to Florida with the three small children, never to be reunited with him.

Charlie's misadventures continued. One evening he was found lying in the middle of a street intersection in a drunken sleep. The police called me to the jail when they were unable to awaken him even with buckets of cold water. I spent a night with him at a hospital with my family internist, listening to obscenities and threats from my son while he came out of his drunken state. By morning he had recovered after a relatively mild case of delirium tremens. He promised to quit drinking. He said he had "learned his lesson."

For another year he traveled from Miami to Chicago and points between, getting jobs and losing them and learning little. On his last Christmas at home he showed up in summer clothes. I bought him some winter things, which he pawned or had stolen from him while drunk. But I still never saw him drunk, only afterward. Later he was admitted and then put out of another treatment center.

Having by then entered the alcoholism field myself, I sought advice from a friend who had been director of Charlie's last treatment center. My friend obtained the records and behind closed doors read me the frightening diagnosis: "sociopathic personality with antisocial tendencies." When I asked what could be done, my friend, a psychiatric social worker and for eight years the director of a reputable alcoholism program, told me: "I don't know. I really don't. They [sociopathic personalities] are the worst kind."

Another friend, a psychiatrist and consultant for Samaritan Center, talked to my son later at my request. Afterward he confirmed both the diagnosis and the prognosis. "He's a sociopathic personality. He doesn't want to change. *Nothing can be done for him if he doesn't want to change.*"

"Nothing can be done for him! He doesn't want to change!" These are the ominous words heard by many another concerned person of an alcoholic. They are frequently spoken by "experts." Who can contradict the family physician in our culture? He has become almost sacred. Few dare to dispute his pronouncements. Everywhere we are advised: "Take only under a doctor's direction"; "As your physician advises"; "Do what your doctor tells you." "Doctor's orders" has become the ultimate qualification for authority. There are thousands of excellent and devoted physicians and other practitioners helping alcoholics but, tragically, there are many others causing damage. This is due to their ignorance and a popular tendency to ascribe erudition to them on almost any aspect of health or illness.

I confronted myself with the dread words "nothing can be done" even though it had been stated by an intelligent, kind, and competent psychiatrist who also understood alcoholism. Then I made a decision. I *would not* and I *did not* accept either the diagnosis of "sociopathic personality" or the prognosis that there was no hope. I would do something on my own just as I had in starting the Samaritan Center about two years earlier. Another knowledgeable professional had frankly told me he did not think I was the proper person to start it. I then made the decision to act in a way that I have since sometimes called "the love cure."

Charlie came home after a brawl in which he suffered a cut lip. The next evening I acted. I sat down with him on the sofa in our living room and made a speech:

"I am putting you out of this house. You are no longer welcome here. You will not come back. I will give you no more money, no clothes, no food, nothing. You must leave now. You must go out and resolve your problem. Find somebody to help you once and for all. You must accept it. You must do it yourself. As matters stand now, you are killing yourself, and I am helping you. Every time I give you money, clothes, bail you out of jail, and get you another job, all I am doing is helping you keep on neglecting your problem. Your problem is alcoholism and until you do something about it, you are not going to succeed at anything." When I finally convinced him that I would not back down one inch he asked me to what treatment facility he should go.

I replied that I did not know. It was true he "had tried them all," as he insisted. He had been in AA. He had gone to a psychiatrist, to a psychiatric center specializing in alcoholism, and to a state psychiatric hospital. He had also been to the Samaritan Center briefly, out of curiosity. He had also consulted a social worker-counselor. All to no avail. I told him it was not they who had failed; it was he who had not persevered. I told him that almost any treatment plan will succeed if continued long enough. I told him that I, his father, could not tell him where to go. One of our problems, I told him, had been that he came to me in the role of a contrite little boy when he wanted help, but then would tell me to go hang myself when he wanted to assert his adult independence. I was cutting myself off. He would have to make his own decisions.

I made one promise. If and when he started "doing something" positive and constructive about his problem, and if he could show me that he was, I would give him all the help possible. I would make any sacrifice to help *after,* I emphasized, he started "doing something" in earnest about his alcoholism.

That night I passed the acid test of chapter 3 that I now commend to others. I told myself: "I love my son enough to give him up forever if that is the only way I can find to make him wake up to the fact that he is killing himself with my help." It is a vital test for parents of alcoholics. That night I put Charlie out of my house. He returned later and I listened to him knocking on the door for what seemed hours. I thought he would never stop. I agonized for hours. But I did not weaken. I did not answer my son's knock.

Two months later he tested my resolve. He had moved into the YMCA and was working as an ice-cream vender for small commissions. He came to see me to borrow money for room rent. I refused him. He then asked for just a quarter for bus fare to get to work the next day. I refused and reminded him of my promises to him. "What do you want me to do?" he asked. (As I have said before, I *never saw him drunk.* Again he was quite sober.) I repeated my admonition: "Do something to help yourself." But I would not tell him what that "something" should be.

He came to see me once more and asked if he might be admitted to the Samaritan Center. I was surprised although I believe that secretly I had hoped that this is what he would do. But I suppressed that thought. I pointed out to him that getting help from one's father in an emotional problem was not recommended by any psychotherapist. I had to admit, however, that since Samaritan Center was partially funded with state money and by public contributions, I could not deny him admission on the grounds that he was my son.

A few days later he visited the center and was checked in. At that time I was not only the director, I was the entire staff. I was the only counselor. My only help came from the clients themselves.

Charlie and I made an agreement that worked. He would, of course, not receive any special treatment, but neither would we try to pretend that he wasn't my son. It is not important to consider what the treatment was at this point. What mattered most is that I made up my mind to insist that Charlie get help and stuck to my resolution. I think he received the message. I loved him enough to risk losing his love if necessary to save him from a surely fatal illness.

Charlie's uninterrupted sobriety began ten years ago. He left the Samaritan Center determined to enter alcoholism work and has remained in it—continuously sober—ever since. He currently is chief counselor at an alcoholism treatment hospital in another state.

Today I advise parents in similar situations to take this same freedom risk with their offspring unless he or she has no familiarity with alcoholism treatment resources. The reason for not guiding them into a previously selected program is that most parents have usually already done too much directing. They need to allow the sick offspring to make his own decision. In most cases the parents, above all others, need to concentrate on cutting the apron strings.

THE MARRIED ALCOHOLIC CHILD

The spouse of an alcoholic is deeply involved in his life and is an essential partner, living and sharing, with similar needs and life expectancies. Parents of alcoholics are in a less strategic position. If the alcoholic is married, it is more appropriate, desirable, and practical for the spouse to use guided intervention. If the marriage has ended permanently—not just technically—then the parents may be able to play a more effective role. But even an estranged wife or husband may return to interfere because he or she has a vested right to do so. Or, there may be a new girl friend or boyfriend. He or she can spoil the whole plan.

Parents must weigh the degree of intimate association they continue to have with their alcoholic offspring. Are they feeding him and even supporting him for all practical purposes? Does he still live with them as my son did? Effective parental intervention will hinge on the amount of viable influence they continue to exert in the life of their sick child. In many, many cases, parents overprotect their sick son or daughter until they too become co-alcoholics just as the wives described earlier.

These parental relationships are recognized by outsiders because it is not common in our culture for parents to continue to support adult children. But the parents who do are the quickest to identify alcoholism as an "illness." They do so so they can justify the unusual support they are giving grown children. But they are in fact aggravating the problem with *co-alcoholism*.

Most parents can succeed if they will persist with the principles of guided intervention. They can refuse to consort with, visit, help, and acknowledge the existence of their married alcoholic offspring. They must treat the alcoholic child and the spouse as a unit. They can tell the person married to their child that if she or he will not take proper steps to help their son, he or she may in fact be helping him kill himself. They can provide them with this book. They can continue "freezing out" the couple in the alcoholic marriage until one partner gets help and starts a positive program of action. To parents of adult alcoholics who argue that they are "helpless" because their sick child is married to someone who will not help, I say: "If that is true, you are handicapped. But there is one thing you *can* do. You can deny them your love, your time, and your attention." You can tell them together: "You two are in a suicide pact. It is so frightening to us, your parents, that we beg you to find help or we must withdraw from both of you. We know we are helping you to continue this insane way of life by trying to play the game of pretending you have an acceptable marriage. We will not play the game. We love our son too much. We love him enough never to see him again if that is what we must do to impress on you, his wife, the great need there is to get help. Please do it so we can renew our normal relationship. We want to love both of you."

If the alcoholic offspring lives at home and has never had a viable outside relationship, the parents may use some of the same step-by-step methods recommended for wives in the previous chapters. But this is rarely the case. In most cases parents will have to take a more drastic kind of action and take it sooner. Our children will understand the deep love that lies behind such drastic action. Finally, when the alcoholic starts a treatment program, parents should offer support and help without qualms as long as the alcoholic continues the program.

Some alcoholics will attempt to play unloved and forlorn children with their parents. But if the parents stick by their promises, the alcoholic will get the message. It may take time. It may take a year or longer. I don't think any parent should ever lose all contact with their alcoholic children. They should remain aware of their whereabouts. They should continue to let the alcoholic know that when the recovery program has begun (not when it is "concluded") they will be ready to help morally and emotionally, if not financially. Parental love, assistance, and cooperation should be withdrawn when the alcoholic discontinues the treatment program. The key is: Help when they work at it, deny help and recognition when they quit. Remember, it is not when he "stops drinking," but when he stops the treatment program, when he stops going to meetings, when he leaves the hospital or treatment center too soon. Stop helping whenever he shows the first signs of thinking he is "cured." There is no cure for alcoholism today.

ALCOHOLIC PARENT

I have had less experience in guided intervention when the concerned persons were children of alcoholic parents than with any other relationships. I have had fewer who have sought my help and who have been able to carry it out. The pressures applied in guided intervention by parents helping an alcoholic adult offspring are almost the same as for children of alcoholic parents. The same questions arise: Are there other persons with closer relationships? Is the nonalcoholic parent still living with the alcoholic? In that case the co-alcoholic parent needs to read this book and that parent needs to be involved. The same is suggested as in the case of parents of adult offspring alcoholics. Treat the alcoholic marriage as a unit. Deny the parents—both of them—your love and recognition as long as the co-alcoholic, as well as the alcoholic, refuses to seek help. The goal again is not for the alcoholic to stop drinking but for the alcoholic to get into a treatment plan.

In using guided intervention with either parents of adult alcoholics or with children of alcoholic parents, the concerned person should tell himself: "As long as I refuse to acknowledge the existence of alcoholism I am aiding and abetting it. I am helping to kill my loved one suffering from alcoholism unless I do everything in my power to get him to accept help. If all else fails, I must withhold the usual demonstrations of love and affection until a helping plan has started. Then I can and should support and help. But if the program is discontinued before final success is achieved—at least two years of uninterrupted sobriety with continuing treatment—then I should withdraw again until the program is resumed."

ALCOHOLIC EMPLOYEE

The most successful application of guided intervention is by employers. In industry, when it has been applied, it is sometimes called "constructive coercion." I first heard it called this in a magazine for federal parole officers where this approach was used successfully by an officer helping an alcoholic ex-prison inmate on parole. All over the United States employers are beginning to intervene with alcoholic employees with much success. Much is being written about industrial alcoholism programs. They are usually a version of guided intervention applied quickly and impersonally by the employer. They are now called "troubled employee" programs to avoid the stigma of applying "alcoholism" or even "problem drinking" to those in the program. But alcohol abuse and alcoholism are known to be a leading cause of absenteeism, reduced production, and of higher costs in most industries. What I write here for the possible "concerned person" employer is more for the small businessman to apply to a single employee or for an individual foreman or supervisor in any establishment.

You, the foreman or boss, already have a good idea that this employee is an alcoholic. You can smell it on his breath. Or, you have noticed how he slows down on Mondays or how long he takes to get back from lunch and then stays away from you because you might smell alcohol on his breath. Or, it may be much more obvious than all that. It may be that this employee has already been involved in more than one traffic violation involving alcohol or that this employee has already been hospitalized for his alcoholism even though he tried to hide the diagnosis with his doctor's unwitting cooperation. It doesn't matter. If you know your employee is an alcoholic, you can proceed.

If you insist that you don't know with certainty, you can proceed just as quickly and effectively. Call your employee into your office and privately confront him. Simply state that you have noticed that he has been absent excessively, or that the quality of his work is suffering, or that he seems to be suffering from a problem that you—since you are not a doctor—cannot identify. All you ask the employee to do is to look into the problem and do something about it.

Such a confrontation is hard for an employee to take, even if alcoholism is not the hidden factor. It is embarrassing and humiliating. It is frightening and threatening to him. The boss doesn't call employees in very often to complain unless their job is really in the balance. Every employee knows this. No matter what the rules or regulations say, no matter what the relationship has been before, when the boss has a private talk and talks about how the employee is doing his job, every employee knows the unspoken words are: change or you may be fired.

Every boss should remember it. He should not feel that he is prying into the employee's personal life, the excuse most bosses use not to apply guided intervention. He must know that there comes a time when it is for the employee's own good that he look into his private life. This becomes true when things happening in his private life have begun to affect his employment. If the boss feels reluctant to talk about the worker's "private affairs," keep the conversation pinpointed to his performance on the job.

What will happen many times is that the employee will immediately confess to the boss that he does have a problem. He may or may not call it by its real name, but refer to it as "nerves" or "problems with his wife" or by some other euphemism. He may even mention alcohol or "drinking a little too much lately." In almost every case the employee will accept the boss's reprimand and not strike back. But the question remains, how to follow up?

If the worker is in fact an alcoholic (and most cases will prove that he is), he may cut down on his drinking enough to avoid the telltale signs that have been noticeable. When employers discover an employee's alcoholism it is usually going to be when the problem has reached the late stages. Alcoholics will fight to preserve their jobs even after they have lost wives, children, and friends. After all, without an income they think they cannot drink. There is also a common myth about alcoholism that keeps them determined to protect their jobs. That is that all alcoholics are bums, lazy, good-time Charleys who are not capable of making a living and holding a job. It follows, they reason, that as long as they hold their jobs they are proving they are not alcoholics. That is why most employers are not going to have any difficulty identifying the alcoholic employee. By the time alcoholism has been able to affect his job enough to be noticed, it will be in an advanced stage.

The follow-up for the alcoholic should come when the earlier symptoms reappear. Anyone can be assured that they will, if he is an alcoholic. At any rate, within a short period of time, the boss can call the "troubled employee" in for a follow-up conference just to inquire. Did he find out what was causing his "nervous" condition? Has he been able to resolve the problems he was having with his wife? Most alcoholics will suspect that the boss knows what his problem really is and will feel threatened by the second meeting even more than by the first.

One suggestion I have for any boss-worker meeting: If the worker hints or mentions alcohol, drinking, or alcoholism, the employer will know his suspicions have been confirmed.

If he mentions AA, group therapy, a hospital for his drinking, or to "get a rest," that gives the employer an opening. He should seize it calmly but firmly. The employee should be told that the boss wants him to go or that he is "expected to go." He may be told that as long as he is going to AA or accepting another treatment program that his "job will be safe" or that it "will be protected." The message will be clear.

If the discussion has taken an open and frank reference to drinking or alcoholism, he may be told that whether he drinks or not is his own business. But when he does anything that begins to cut down on his ability to perform or that interferes with his work, it becomes the employer's concern. The worker can be told that alcoholism is a disease (if the employer believes that it is) and that the employer understands it as a problem that requires outside help. To encourage him to talk about it, references can be made to some successful person known to both boss and worker whose alcoholism has been arrested. Make it clear that the employer is *not* seeking proof that the employee is no longer drinking. Make it clear that what is sought is only evidence that he is pursuing a solution to his problem by going to AA meetings or by another kind of treatment for alcoholics. The distinction between getting the alcoholic to "stop drinking" and to "do something" about his problem is just as important as it is for a relative of an alcoholic. The name of the game is *not* "stop what you are doing" but "*start* doing something."

An employer can pursue the alcoholic with greater assurance of success than a relative or loved one. His relationship is not an intimate one. It is a business relationship. He is paying money to this person in return for certain services. When the worker fails to deliver these services the boss has an obligation to himself and to many others not to ignore the problem.

If more humanitarian considerations are needed, the employer can be assured that he is in a position to help the alcoholic employee probably quicker, easier, and with less lost motion than anyone else in that stricken man's world. I have found many employers too timid to make demands on their poor alcoholic workers until the alcoholic breaks the camel's back with that final straw. Then they have fired them just as the "timid" wives have obtained divorces from supposedly dominant alcoholic husbands after reaching their breaking point. It is better for both parties to bite the bullet and force the issue early. Early treatment can change the whole picture; late treatment can be futile. It could be the alcoholic's last job.

Anyone in a position of influence with an alcoholic can, by applying the pressure he has available, help to get the alcoholic into treatment and keep him there. If the relationship is not the most intimate in the alcoholic's life—or if other people tend to interfere—it is still worth the effort. Even an employer whose alcoholic employee removes himself from the employer's influence by quitting his job can help by calling the wife or another appropriate concerned person. He might explain to this person why the alcoholic has quit. He might explain that he still values the alcoholic employee's services, that he was trying to get the alcoholic to accept treatment. Such a telephone call or personal communication between a wife and an employer could save years of misery and tragedy for the alcoholic. Remember, alcoholics are usually dependent and sensitive people. Their employers, parents, marriage partners, and children are more important to them than they might be to a nonalcoholic. That's one reason intelligent application of guided intervention works.

8

Achieving Success with Guided Intervention

Your goal is that your alcoholic stay in a treatment program for two years, staying sober at the same time without interruption. When he has begun to do that you are almost certain of success. This chapter deals with the problems of keeping him in treatment and getting him back if he quits.

If you have been able to follow the guided intervention techniques to this point, the follow-ups will come easier. Briefly, let us review the steps. You have a counselor to guide you. Then you have also brought to your home a preliminary quieting of the atmosphere. You have stopped all nagging, fussing, crying, and threatening. You also stopped pouring liquor down the drain, hunting for bottles, and getting upset each time he went to buy some.

You have been able to apply the "feather touch" first step, announcing to him that you, yourself, were going to a counselor or to AA or to Al-Anon. You continued to go and to make the announcement, before and after going. You continued avoiding arguments, avoiding any temptation to persuade him to go with you, but always leaving the door open for him to go with you if he wanted to. You refused any attempts by him to get you into discussions about the merits of what you were doing or whether he was truly an "alcoholic" or any other argument. You kept your mind on your first goal: to get him to start the program. You avoided previous ill-advised attempts to get him to stop drinking. Finally, he accepted and started going to the counseling sessions with you or to AA while you went to Al-Anon. So now what?

First, be forewarned that almost every alcoholic who starts any treatment has at least one more drinking episode before he finally succeeds in finding recovery. But a drinking experience should not be considered a sign of failure. The way you react to this event will help your alcoholic to accept it. It is only a temporary setback. It should not discourage him or you from continuing the program. Since it will depend very much on you, prepare yourself and don't think the end of the world has come when it happens.

Perhaps I am ahead of myself. Many alcoholics continue drinking even after they start accepting a program. In guided intervention it is even more likely. But eventually all alcoholics will stop. You need to be patient. You need to believe in the plan. Alcoholics find it nearly impossible to continue the same drinking level after they start going to counseling, group meetings, or AA. But if they continue drinking, it is usually at a reduced rate. If you, the concerned person, handle yourself intelligently and lovingly, he will eventually stop drinking on his own time. You do not have to tell him. But even after he doesn't drink for many weeks or months, the odds are that he will have at least one more drinking episode. When it happens you need patience, love, and understanding. You should have come to accept that his problem is beyond your alcoholic's ability to resolve alone. And it is impossible for you to force a solution on him. When he drinks again you need to convince him that there is no reason for him to feel defeated. Assure him that you don't, and assure him that you appreciate the difficulty he has been having, that you admire the strength he has shown you throughout the ordeal of abstinence. Assure him of your love. Assure him of your confidence in him. (Alcoholics suffer from very low self-esteem.) He needs more loving and reassurance than someone else might. Have faith for both of you and transfer this faith to him. You will both need it.

There is another problem that occurs frequently in the intervention process. Even after he gets involved in the treatment process he will likely reach a point in which he quits it. He may quit after a few weeks because he has not been able to stop drinking. If you have continued fussing and badgering him, he is even more quickly discouraged. Even if you have been able to follow my advice in your actions and words, he may yet have been able to pick up your true feelings from your facial expressions, the telltale way you slammed doors or cleared your throat, and other things in which you gave away your true feelings. If you have done much of this, and your alcoholic has not been able to stop drinking, he is likely to quit the program and tell you, "It is no use. I can't do it. You can see I've tried. I just can't." But even if you have done everything letter perfect, he may quit the program because of the gigantic problem it is for him. Don't be discouraged.

There is another reason your alcoholic may quit the program, the exact opposite of the first. He does quit drinking. He gets sober and stays sober for an impressive length of time. For one this may be three or four weeks. For another, it may be two or three months. Neither has any great meaning. Neither is enough. Even if he stops for a period of one or two years, if he does not accept some kind of treatment at the same time, the prognosis is poor, very poor. But it gives your alcoholic an ostensible "reasonable" kind of excuse. "What's the point of all these meetings? Nothing really happens. After you have heard one of these sob stories, you have heard them all." The alcoholic's arguments seem to "make sense," but making sense is not the criteria of success.

The program must be continued at all costs. No argument to quit can be acceptable. The plan goes on. The first follow-up rule for a quitter is simple: Do the same thing you did to get him to start. If it took two or three weeks to get him to start going to the meetings or the counselor, then do the same things again. Your reactions to his discontinuing the program should be the same as they were when he would not hear or respond to your quiet repeated invitations. Surprisingly, the same procedures will work again. When he stops going, no matter what he says, the fact is that he is probably stopping because he needs to return directly to his alcohol or he needs to return to the more permissive environment that will eventually let him drink again. He finds it intolerable, if not impossible, to continue drinking while he is hearing all those unpleasant stories at AA about drinking. He finds he dislikes himself more when he continues to hear from others like himself who tell over and over how happy they are now *not drinking*. He gets to the point that he wants to tell them to shut up, to stop telling him what's wrong about drinking. If he is going to group therapy with you and other wives and husbands of nonalcoholics, he finds it intolerable to keep hearing from other concerned persons how different and happy their lives are when their alcoholic stops drinking. All these things hit him as a barrage of goodie-goodie talk. He "knows" he's a "bad person," and he cannot see himself any other way. He knows that if he accepts what these other people are telling him, he will have to join them and that will mean "not drinking," and that is still completely impossible for him to accept. His view of his future must involve alcohol. He cannot endure to think of himself as ever shut off from alcohol. It has got to be present and available to him. Not to have it for the rest of his life is as unthinkable as not having food, water, and air. So he rejects the meetings, the counseling sessions out of fear. He has been tempted to accept them. These happy people who say they were like he is now might be telling the truth. And he feels he cannot be like them. He still feels—in his gut—that without alcohol life is not worth living. This is why alcoholics quit treatment plans. This is why they refuse to talk to counselors or recovered alcoholics from AA. When they agree, deep inside they harbor secret escape plans. They attend but they don't listen. They don't hear. They cannot apply to themselves what they have been told. They do not believe. They go only to please their concerned person. They go because you have quietly enticed them. They are not going with open minds. They go under compulsion and they don't like it. It is not surprising when they stop going. It should be more surprising when they continue going and respond. That's a bigger mystery for us who are experienced. When the first setback comes it may be a signal that something is about to penetrate their alcoholic defenses. Seeing that something about to score, about to show him that there might be some sense, some hope, his innermost self—his deep, unconscious alcoholic mind—starts screaming "no!" at him. His alcoholic devil begins to protest: Don't keep this up or you are going to lost your appreciation for me, your magic medicine, your only reliable friend, don't do it!

When this setback occurs, be understanding. Continue to go and to invite him, but *do not persuade.* Your going yourself and even your gentle subtle invitations hit him as screams! Don't make it harder by adding words. Do keep it up. Do not relent.

However, you should not wait again as long as you waited the first time. If you possibly can, set a limit on the number of days you will wait. Assume that he thought the program had something to offer if he went at all. Assume that it was helpful. The pressures applied to him were increased very slowly. If he went to group therapy, then he may not have been pressured at first unless he was a big talker and came in ready to "teach" the group. He might have been confronted with his alcoholism too quickly. He may have been pushed too soon. It doesn't matter. When the confrontations occur early in groups for alcoholics, the result is usually a long rest period for the newcomer. Whatever happens in the group or at the AA meeting, he can find a good reason for discontinuing it whenever he wants to find one.

I sincerely believe that even the most seemingly mature alcoholic in the early part of a program has to be treated like a child insofar as the program is concerned. Children find the conflict between teacher pressure and the unprecedented peer pressure from children of their own size and age almost intolerable. It can be terrifying. The alcoholic in his first AA meeting may find the stark-naked truth-telling of other alcoholics—hearing out loud what he has been secretly thinking and feeling—too hard, too threatening to his plans of never quitting. He may identify too strongly with the speakers. Seeing himself on the speaker's rostrum, telling the whole world his own deep, dark secrets, is an assault on his fantasy world. How is he going to hang on to his delusion of not being able to live without his liquor? That's the threat the alcoholic may feel after his first AA meeting. The common complaint of alcoholics who reject AA is that they get tired of "those stories about drinking." "I don't see how hearing about drinking and getting drunk can help me," your alcoholic may tell you. What he doesn't know is that it isn't "hearing the words" that helps but "hearing" the feelings. It takes the alcoholic longer to understand that.

In group therapy his experience may have been even more excruciating. The confrontations in AA happen slowly and indirectly. In group therapy the process is speeded up, and he may experience his first vicarious confrontation by witnessing one in the group. Identifying himself with another alcoholic who is being confronted will be more threatening than an AA speaker's story.

You, the advocate of the meetings, must remember to expect these reactions before you start. They can be overcome. Your alcoholic needs the help and will return even if he at first rejects it with firm determination.

If, after a week or two, he persists in not returning, it may be time to go into a second phase. You and your counselor should decide at what point to start the new phase. It may be only days. It may be weeks. In unusual circumstances—your feelings and strength—it could run for several weeks. When he started and later quit, he tacitly demonstrated that he felt he needed help or he would not have gone. The fact that he stopped is more often a sign the therapy was reaching him, not that it wasn't. He might continue a program that didn't "hurt"—one that meant little or nothing to him—if it brought peace and quiet at home. You should give him peace and quiet at home while he continues in the program. So when he refuses to continue going it can be taken as a sign that it was beginning to be more than a neutral indifferent experience for him.

There are different ways of increasing the pressure after the simple announcements and invitations have failed. Until now you have merely left the door open for him—even after he started going and then stopped—without trying to push him through the door, so to speak. Now the time may have come for increasing this pressure. The simplest way is to make the words a little stronger. Instead of merely inviting him on an "if-you-want-to" basis, you make the message direct and clear. But first announce as you did before that you have something "important" you want to say. Then say something like this:

"All right, Jim. Up until now I've never tried to persuade you to go with me. I tried to let you come if and when you felt like it. I tried not to push you or to cajole you. I tried to respect your freedom and your right to make up your own mind. But things have changed a little.

"You have been to the sessions. You have seen what it is. You have seen how it helps other people. It has helped me. But you have stopped and I must insist, Jim, come back. Not for my sake, but for your sake as well as mine. Because we, Jim, you and I, have a problem. And it is going to take both of us to solve it. I am asking you, please, to start coming to these sessions again. Please come back to the sessions. That's all I am asking of you, Jim. Just come to these meetings."

This speech can be longer or shorter. It should be carefully rehearsed with your counselor. The time to make it needs to be set in advance. As in the first announcement, it should be made when he is cold sober. It should be made when there is little chance of interruption. It should be made when he can give you his attention. It should be made only once. It should not be repeated. To be memorable, an experience has to have a singular quality. If it is repeated, it loses its potency. The words lose power. Repetition dilutes the message. He should hear these heartfelt words from you only once. Speak them clearly and with feeling. Get them out of your system once and for all.

The thing that will distinguish this speech from others that may follow is that it will make no threat; no ultimatum will be issued. You have relied strictly on trying to communicate your sadness, your near despair. You have pleaded for understanding, but you have not mentioned any possible unpleasant alternative. After making the speech, you should stop. Allow it to sink in. Do not demand an answer. Don't be tricked into a long discussion of his problems or yours. Don't discuss the pros and cons. You are asking very little of him—only that he *go to the sessions.* Deep in your heart you they have helped. Deep inside you, you know they were beginning to help him. So stick with your original resolution. Please, come with me, you say. But come with you or not, you are going to continue to go. And you do.

Only time will tell if your alcoholic will return to the program. Once again, after making your long speech, wait. Discontinue your invitations. All you do now is to leave the door open. But give him the time and the opportunity to pick up from where you left him. Let him make up his mind. Give him time to show that he heard you and that he is accepting your plea. You and your counselor should decide how long to wait. A shorter wait than you gave him the first time should be allowed before proceeding to another phase. But after the deadline that you and your counselor have set has passed, you are ready for another turn of the screw.

DOORBELL INTERVENTION

You have reached a point that calls for a decision on the direction your pressure is leading. It should be either toward a quasi-legal intervention or using your counselor or another third party to intervene for you. The quasi-legal intervention is more threatening than the counselor intervention. It can always be used as a follow-up to the counselor intervention. To use the counselor after the lawyer would tend to weaken the effect. You and your counselor should discuss the alternatives and decide which one seems more suitable and most promising of success with your alcoholic. If your counselor is willing, I recommend using the counselor first.

After you have waited a predetermined time—be sure you do not lull yourself into indifference and get off a schedule—make a second speech. This one is much shorter. It assumes that your follow-up will be to use your counselor to intervene later if necessary. It may not be necessary.

Your short speech should sound something like this:

"Jim, I am going to give you until Monday, the 15th, to come back to the sessions with me. If you don't, then I'll have to do *something else.*"

That is all you say. Again you have said it when you know he could hear it all. Say it just once. Do not allow him to get you into an argument. Do not add to it or take away from it by making a response to any verbal abuse. Do not let him persuade you to back down no matter what he threatens or does. No matter whether he goes on the biggest bender of the year or stays away from you for the longest time ever or abuses you, stick to your plan.

If his response is to ask what the "something else" might be, don't take the bait. This is not a question in good faith. It is a play. Tell him you are not sure. You really don't know. If you think it won't make matters worse, simply repeat the message in the same words: "You have until Monday, the 15th, to come back to the sessions with me. If you don't then I'll have to do *something else.*" Let the ominous possibilities of that "something else" sink in. Let him worry a little bit about it. But don't discuss, argue, cajole, or nag. After the idea has registered with him, drop the subject. He will get the message.

If, after giving him the "something else" notice, he does not respond—and it is surprising how many will succumb—you are ready for your counselor's help: the doorbell intervention.

You and your counselor agree on a good time to find your alcoholic sober and with some time on his hands. In my experience the time has usually been a Sunday morning. Sunday morning is usually a time of relaxation. Some may be going to church but it is usually easy to have church postponed. In most of my cases, going to church has been a thing of the past. After setting the time and date, arrange for no one to be home but you and your alcoholic. If there are children, make plans so they can be away spending the night with friends or relatives. Have the house quiet and peaceful. Choose the time of morning your alcoholic will be most receptive. It may be a little while after breakfast. I have always planned the exact time to come knocking at the door. At the appointed time the wife should be in the backyard or further away from the front door than the alcoholic. If it is easier for you, you, the concerned person, may choose not be be at home. This is a decision that only you can make. I find it helpful to have the wife available in the house. Let the alcoholic at the appropriate time decide if he wants to talk alone or with his wife present. This is something to decide in conference with your counselor. The counselor's own preference plays a part, too. If the counselor is a professional in alcoholism, he should be able to meet the preferences of the concerned person. After the plans have been made, the final arrangement should be that unless you telephone the counselor because of an unforeseen event, the counselor will be there.

An experienced counselor will not need many directions. An AA member who has made Twelfth Step* calls will know how to handle himself. I have approached doorbell interventions over the past several years with something less than enthusiasm since in most cases the alcoholic has been rejecting all help and mine in particular. But in almost all these encounters I have left feeling happy and excited because I have seen the alcoholic do a complete turnabout. I now recommend the doorbell intervention with enthusiasm because it is one of the most useful tools I have found in reaching a reluctant alcoholic. I daresay many successful interventions by AA members have begun with visits similar to mine. But it is not recommended with an alcoholic who is not sober. It also requires the full cooperation of the concerned person.

It is eight o'clock on the Sunday morning that you agreed upon for your cooperating counselor to come. You don't tell your alcoholic anything in advance. That is part of the technique. If you tell him, he may very well find an excuse not to

*When AA members call on an alcoholic in trouble they refer to such action as working the Twelfth Step, which calls for them to carry the message of AA to other alcoholics.

be home by going fishing or to church. Or, he may just do what he would have the technical right to do, he might say he did not care to meet and talk with your counselor. Don't tell him in advance. Let it come as a surprise.

I have stood on many a front porch on a Sunday morning and rang the doorbell and waited nervously for my "target" to answer the door. The wait has been nerve-racking, but usually not long. The alcoholic, frequently in his bathrobe, has answered the door, wondering who I was. I have a graying beard about which he has usually heard. He has usually known my name and sometimes my face. After he has opened the door, I have spoken quickly, usually calling him by his first name, instead of the formal "mister."

"Jim Brown?" I ask, opening the informality quickly.

"Yes, I'm Jim Brown."

"I'm Roque Fajardo, " I say, offering my hand.

In almost every instance, my frightened alcoholic quarry melts immediately and invites me inside. In the rare cases when he does not quickly ask me to come in, I say: "I came by to talk with you a few minutes, if I may." This is enough to get the invitation. If it isn't I add, "May I come in?" I have never been refused.

In most cases I do not have to start the conversation. In most cases the alcoholic has his curiosity so whetted by unanswered questions by his wife that he starts talking and asking questions easily. A good counselor will know how to handle this. He will permit the alcoholic to carry the ball all the way, if possible. He will respond to the alcoholic's needs and questions and will let him set the pace, the tone, and the length of the interview.

If the alcoholic is timid and will not volunteer conversation, the counselor should proceed quietly and nonthreateningly to introduce himself and his attitudes about meeting the alcoholic and about people. He should apologize early for the unannounced surprise visit. Perhaps, too, if the alcoholic is timid, the wife should find her way into the meeting with his permission or by his invitation or at the counselor's suggestion. Having the wife present may help the alcoholic to overcome his fear and embarrassment.

It is best for the counselor not to discuss alcoholism, drinking, or alcoholics unless the alcoholic himself broaches the subject. He usually will. The counselor should not linger on the subject even if it is introduced but should get to the basic reason for his call: to get the alcoholic *to come to counseling sessions or to AA meetings* or whatever was planned. He should extend the invitation openly and simply. The alcoholic will interpret—correctly—the counselor's visit as a big meaningful step, the "something else" the wife promised. It, therefore, does not need to be spelled out any further.

In my doorbell interventions, the alcoholic has been anxious to talk with me at length. In most cases I have had to adjourn the visit myself after about two hours since I don't relish Sunday morning work. But I have left each time with an appointment with the alcoholic in my office. Many who came after the doorbell intervention later required other pressures and other inducements. But once an alcoholic has taken the first or second steps toward getting into treatment he can be returned to it later if he falters along the way.

QUASI-LEGAL MOVE

If doorbell intervention does not get results or if after getting started the alcoholic backtracks and a new turn of the screw is called for, the quasi-legal procedure is next.

When that point is reached careful planning is called for again. Your first quasi-legal step is identical to the one that preceded the doorbell intervention. This time, instead of saying "something else," you say, "see a lawyer." Your full speech should be similar to this:

"Jim, I am going to give you until Thursday, the 18th, to come back with me to the sessions. If you don't, I am going *to see a lawyer.*"

I call this quasi-legal because it doesn't employ court action. But it is a strong threat to your alcoholic. If he thought you were not serious before, he may now see it differently. By "seeing a lawyer" you open the way for a court action restraining his conduct, a legal separation, a divorce, or even legal commitment of him to a treatment facility or hospital. He will get the message in most cases without your drawing him a picture. Again, don't let him get you into a discussion of why you want to see a lawyer or whether you will seek a divorce or separation or anything else. Leave him guessing. All you have asked is that he *come to some meetings.* This certainly is easy for anyone. If he loves you and wants to keep you, the chances are good that he will heed this ultimatum and start whatever you ask.

You are doing this because you love your alcoholic enough that you will leave him if that is what is required to wake him up to his self-destructive behavior. Fail to act and your alcoholic is going to get worse until he dies in an accident, is maimed for life, loses his ability to work, or succumbs to brain damage or cirrhosis of the liver. The compromise in-between option is just as unpromising. But if you can guide him into accepting help, your life, his life, and your children's lives can be changed dramatically as they have been changed for millions of others.

After giving the lawyer-visit speech, you must follow through on schedule *by seeing the lawyer* if your sick one has not responded. In choosing a lawyer—he should be chosen in advance—I would suggest you get help from your alcoholism counselor. The lawyer need not be a divorce lawyer or even a lawyer who would eventually handle a divorce. Choose a lawyer who will cooperate most willingly with the procedures we outline. If there is time, let the lawyer peruse this book long enough to cover this chapter. Make certain that you do *not* go to a lawyer who is going to try to push you into a *divorce.* Good attorneys, just as good professionals in all fields, won't do that. But some attorneys have a black-and-white view of alcoholism and having heard of your failures to have your alcholic do something as simple as go to meetings, an attorney in good conscience may try to urge you to give up and proceed with a divorce. This is *not* the advice you need now. Divorce, or even separation, is *not* your goal. Your goal is only that your sick husband respond to help. That is all. Make certain the lawyer you get understands this.

When you get a lawyer willing to cooperate with your plans ask him to write a letter for you to your husband. The letter should be on the lawyer's letterhead. The letterhead is the strongest factor. The letter should read like this:

SMITH AND SMITH
Attorneys-at-Law
1010 Main Street Building
Cityville, Your State
January 10, 1976

Dear Mr. Brown:

Your wife, Mary Brown, has asked me to intercede for her in a matter of great importance to her. She states that you and she have received counseling help from Mr. Bill Jones, an alcholism counselor, at the Cityville Center. But you have discontinued going to the sessions and group meetings at great peril to your welfare.

Mrs. Brown feels that these meetings are important to her, to you, and to your marriage. She is most anxious that you resume going to the sessions. This letter is to ask you to resume your attendance at these sessions.

I would appreciate hearing from you saying that you will resume attending the sessions. Your cooperation in this matter would be appreciated by me and Mrs. Brown.

Yours very truly,
John M. Smith

Note that the letter does not mention any other action. It is not necessary. The fact that the letter comes from an attorney, that it is a written message on an attorney's letterhead, and that an attorney has become involved will pack a strong message. In most cases the single letter does the job. A deadline should be agreed on by the lawyer, you, and your counselor in advance. When it is reached a second letter should be sent. The second one should read like this:

SMITH AND SMITH
Attorneys-at-Law
1010 Main Street Building
Cityville, Your State
January 20, 1976

Dear Mr. Brown:

On behalf of your wife, Mary Brown, we wrote you a

letter on January 10, 1976. Mrs. Brown had asked us to intercede with you in a matter of utmost importance to her and, in her opinion, to you. She asked that you resume attending counseling sessions with Mr. Bill Jones at the Cityville Center. Mrs. Brown feels that your attendance at these meetings has been of help to both of you and that it is most important that they are continued.

Since we have not had the courtesy of a reply to our letter of January 10, we are writing once more to repeat our request. Mrs. Brown asks that you resume these meetings by no later than January 31 so that further action can be avoided.

We hope that you will comply with this simple but important matter that Mrs. Brown is convinced is so vital to yourself, to her, your family, and your marriage. She is anxious to avoid further action.

You are asked to act before January 31.

Yours very truly,
John M. Smith

If the new deadline arrives without a satisfactory response, then your alcoholism and legal counselors need to make plans for your next step. In the cases I have been involved in, the next step has been separation. The wife has demanded that the husband move out or she herself has moved out. The circumstances vary but you should not *under any circumstances* fail to act. None of the steps should be taken unless you are prepared to carry them out. To promise such an action and not to follow through is much more *harmful* than not to act on it in the first place. Never threaten "other action" unless you have real "other action" in mind. When the time comes, take the action.

Most alcoholics are going to respond to your requests long before it has progressed to this point. But a few will wait. Some alcoholics won't respond until the physical pain, the real absence of the wife, or some other tangible event has hit him. For these cases we have no choice. We must be prepared to follow through. Many thousands of alcoholics have not been moved until the wife did move out. Leading up to the event, step by step, will avoid an actual separation if it can be avoided. Many men will not believe that their wives actually will move. Many have heard threats that never materialized so they won't believe it until it happens. The wife's actual moving is often needed before the alcoholic responds. If that is your experience make certain that the threat of "other action" doesn't turn out to be empty. Empty threats hurt everyone concerned by adding to the failures and setbacks, bitterness and hostility.

TEMPORARY SEPARATION

If a separation is carried out, a new deadline should be set for the alcoholic to return to the treatment plan. But this time his return to the plan needs to be firmly established before you return to your home. One month's separation would be an average time. You might have a different view. But it would be most unwise to return too early. To return as soon as your alcoholic resumes the meetings would give him an opportunity to play a game with you by discontinuing them soon after you move back. Once you have moved out of the house—a difficult and traumatic task— you should get full value for your trouble. Convince your alcoholic at a *feeling level*—let him feel your absence for a few weeks—that you are serious, that you are capable of moving out and leaving him. Let him know that his problem is a matter of *life and death,* a matter of *losing you* or of *keeping you.*

Most cases will not reach the separation stage. But when they have they have been successful for me. If the alcoholic goes to the trouble of getting a lawyer himself—many will, of course, as is their right—it is usually no more than another manipulation. You have not threatened divorce. You have not even threatened separation. Your lawyer might have had another idea that might work. But it should not be a threat so big your alcoholic needs an attorney. What has he been asked to do? *Merely that he attend some meetings.* That is all. You will note that the letters did not even mention his drinking. It might be advisable to avoid even the word "alcoholism." But under no circumstances should any stronger threat be made or any allegation be made about your alcoholic's drinking. Your letter asked only that he accept help, to do something positive. He really should not need a lawyer to respond.

If your actions end up in an exchange of actions and counteractions between lawyers, it will have been because you had the wrong lawyer—who did not understand your goal—or your alcoholic husband has fallen into the hands of a poor legal adviser. Keep that in mind before you let the matter get out of hand. This is one of the very important reasons you should have the counsel of an alcoholism counselor as well as legal advice.

Preservation of your marriage is one of your goals. But if legal action should threaten your marriage, it might be that your marriage was not very stable and would not have survived except at the continued expense of your emotional and physical health. I have found alcoholic marriages usually repairable unions once the basic culprit—the alcoholism—has been brought under control.

Always be certain that you are prepared to follow through before you take any step. Plan each step with your counselor. Be prepared for the second step each time you take a first one. Separation is rarely needed but when it is, it will usually succeed in doing the job. If your religion influences your thinking in separation, talk it over with your pastor. Most pastoral counselors are going to understand and approve of guided intervention.

One more word on separations. This separation is not a permanent change in your marital relationship. It is not a prelude to divorce. It is not by any means to be treated as suggesting a lack of love or interest in your marriage partner. Your separation is a tool and a maneuver in the interest of your beloved alcoholic's survival. It follows that it is in the interest of saving your precious marriage, too.

Maintain a practical and objective attitude with your alcoholic without expressing *any less love* for him at a feeling level. Look at him and express with words—if that is your style—the feeling message:

"I love you very much, my husband, but I am not going to let that love cause me to stand by while you are destroying yourself and refusing to do anything about it. I mean to stick by this separation and even to make it permanent if you continue to refuse all help."

There should be no kissing and hugging, absolutely no sexual activity, and no prolonged conversations that tend to foster the alcoholic's inactivity. There should be enough communication to help the alcoholic get to therapeutic activities such as counseling, AA, and group therapy. Above all, there must be a demonstration of continuing and honest involvement by the alcoholic for *at least* one full month before a reunion takes place.

In judging the gut-level honesty of the alcoholic's response to the separation, his personality and previous relationship to the concerned person must be taken into account. If he was the dominant member of the marriage in most things, the response to him needs to be firmer and hard-lined. If he was less dominant in the marriage than the wife, this must be considered in judging his responses. Mathematical formulas in human relationships are not reliable. My advice during the separation is to consult closely with your alcoholism counselor, particularly if his advice has proven good in the past. And don't shut out your heart.

Recently during the separation of a wife-client of mine in another city, she made a decision that contradicted our previous plans. The separation was in its second month, her alcoholic husband was responding with much AA activity and involvement. My client—I'll call her Susan—was the dominant person in the marriage. On a weekend George, the husband, telephoned her. He had broken his sobriety. He was not yet drunk but he had obtained some "courage" from the bottle. George told Susan that he was tired of the separation. He wanted her back. He wanted her back quickly. If she didn't come back, he told her she could "forget it."

This message by a previously dominant man could have been safely interpreted as a plain and simple manipulation, another in a series. But coming from George, who had been patient and dominated most of the time, it was interpreted by Susan as a "cry for help," a genuine and honest plea. She felt she could identify it from the book *I'll Quit Tomorrow* by Vernon E. Johnson. She responded as her heart and mind together dictated and returned home the next day. I believe she made the right decision.

There were three significant factors to remember here. 1) George was not in the habit of issuing ultimatums; he was more commonly on the receiving end of them. 2) George had already given significant evidence of his sincerity by his AA activity and involvement. He accepted chairmanship of his AA group for the first time, having always declined it in the past. He had also taken his Fifth Step, which is usually an important traumatic experience in which an alcoholic admits to God, to himself, and to another human being "the exact nature of (his) wrongs." 3) The separation was almost two months long. Susan had demonstrated plainly and convincingly that she was prepared to insist on his continuing in their treatment plan.

I believe George and Susan's marriage will survive. I believe George has started his final recovery from alcoholism. I believe you and yours can do the same.

9

Why Alcoholics Do What They Do

Alcoholics do the shocking and surprising things they do because their need for alcohol becomes so centrally important in their lives that eventually almost all their behavior is influenced directly or indirectly toward not letting anything or anyone deprive them of it. Alcohol addiction is comparable only with addiction to one of the three opiates—morphine, heroin, and opium. But because a majority of drinkers continue drinking without becoming addicts, the difference in the alcohol addict is almost incomprehensible to the nonalcoholic or social drinker. When the alcoholic happens to be a loved one with whom we have experienced a normal relationship, from whom we have received strength and inspiration, and to whom we have given love and respect, we tend to resist acceptance of the addict's condition with vehemence. In addition, alcoholics themselves resist even more accepting themselves as addicts. They expend much emotional energy hiding their feelings about alcohol from themselves and, most importantly, hiding their condition from those persons closest to them as long as they can.

More simply put, alcoholics do the things they do because of their addiction, a compulsive drive that takes precedence almost over every other human need. The principal reason it is so difficult for us to understand is simply that everything about it and about us is programmed for rejecting it. It is a truth pill too bitter to take without a struggle.

Exactly why drinker "A" becomes an alcoholic and drinker "B" doesn't is not known. Almost all alcohologists are agreed that there seems to be a combination of factors—physical, psychological, and environmental. Many of us believe that some organic, biological condition, either developed or acquired, plays a leading role in the problem. Biochemists have found similarities between the opiates and alcohol in animal brains too technical and esoteric for me to deal with here.* But I believe that sometimes an almost purely "physical craving" is the only explanation I have been able to see in otherwise well-balanced and seemingly mature alcoholics. These have been the exception, however, and like most others in treatment I have long since stopped looking for a simple physical explanation that might delay proper treatment for years or a lifetime and be a disastrous distraction.

Although I believe the physical factor may be the eventual key to the problem, as a therapist I cannot deal with it and succeed in my goal of helping alcoholics needing my help today.

As for the environmental or sociological factor in alcohol addiction, there is little question. Persons reared in an environment that condemns drunkenness and overindulgence but

*"Tests Show Drink Effect on the Mind," report on work of Dr. Michael Collins and Gerald Cohen. *The New York Times,* September 14, 1968, p. 33, and "Alcohol, Amines, and Alkaloids: A Possible Biochemical Basis for Alcohol Addiction," by Virginia C. Davis and Michael J. Walsh, *Science,* February 13, 1970.

not drinking itself less often become alcoholics than those reared in environments where ambivalence about drinking and drunkenness prevails. If you are thinking that your alcoholic's environment condemned drunkenness and overindulgence, recall the implied challenge to manhood in the popular phrases, "drink him under the table!" "carries his liquor like a gentleman!" or, the harmless sounding euphemisms for getting drunk, "one too many," "getting a buzz-on," "a little high," or the Irish tolerance for alcoholism as "the good man's sickness." In addition to this, persons brought up in cultures that dignify the family and encourage strong familial relationships also seem less likely to develop alcoholism. Chinese, Orthodox Jews, and Italians seem to demonstrate these factors by their low alcoholism rates.* On the other hand, when these same factors are removed from any culture or the opposite values are encouraged, the rate of alcoholism rises.

Guided intervention is local application of strong environmental influence to an alcoholic situation. To the extent that it involves only a single concerned person, it is more psychological and interpersonal than sociological. But when a whole family can become involved it takes on a more pervading and an almost sociological aspect.† The sociological nature of the problem needs to be met by changing the attitudes of families, changing our entire culture. How long this will take I do not know. I do know that religious, educational, social, and governmental resources will need to become involved. Until that time arrives, the locally applied pseudo-environmental changes can be instituted by individuals in response to local and singular emergency situations using guided intervention.

The last of the three factors involved in the making of an alcoholic is psychological—the emotional and behavioral problems that may have played a part. To understand psychology today a lay person seeking to solve an alcoholism problem should be made aware that there are two divergent

***Alcohol Education for Classroom and Community,* Raymond & McCarthy, editors, McGraw-Hill, 1969.

†See "A Family Systems Approach to Alcoholism" by Murray Bowen, M.D. Pamphlet reprinted by Charlotte Council on Alcoholism, Inc., 101 Billingsley Road, Charlotte, North Carolina 28211, for a similar approach.

approaches in psychology and that in the area of alcoholism treatment they sometimes hardly speak to one another. One puts all the emphasis on what is happening inside a person. It is usually called dynamic psychology. The other psychologists are the behaviorists, who put their trust in studying what a person does rather than what he thinks or "feels." It may be said that the dynamic psychologist believes man *does* what he is while the behaviorist believes man *is* what he does. The behaviorists claim they are more scientific because they deal only in facts, in measurable quantities of visible behaviors such as how many times a creature performs a certain act and how that relates to other behaviors. What some overlook is that no one knows for sure what anyone is thinking or feeling and that since there is a direct relationship between the two, measuring behavior will always be suspect if we cannot measure "thought" or "feeling" at the same time.

I believe the best treatment for alcoholism should involve both approaches, which is what we have tried to do in developing guided intervention and the treatment modalities at Samaritan Center.

No one has yet demonstrated a prealcoholic psychological personality. But almost all psychological theories of human growth make sense when they are coupled with a simultaneous development of alcohol addiction. You need only inject the premise that at a particular point your alcoholic started ingesting alcohol, and as psychological problems developed, his dependence on alcohol relief increased until addiction occurred. How long alcohol consumption had to occur differs from one person to another. It also remains clear that no specific pattern of behavior invariably results in alcohol addiction except for its repeated or excessive use. Even that does not invariably result in alcoholism.

To understand the general human condition in terms of thought, feeling, and behavior, consider one theory of how we become the person we are. This theory has us starting life with an inferiority complex because of the literally helpless condition in which we humans begin life.*

Life begins in a perfect environment inside our mother's

**I'm OK—You're OK, A Practical Guide to Transactional Analysis* by Thomas A. Harris, Harper & Row, New York.

womb. We float, effortlessly fed, effortlessly oxygenated, and with perfect temperature controls. Then a great traumatic experience occurs: We are born! Suddenly, we are forcibly pushed or pulled from our warm water-cushioned place into a hard, cold world. Our automatic oxygen is cut off and we are forced to breathe with our nose and lungs for the first time. Within seconds we discover we are at the mercy of some giants who control everything: our food, the temperatures, our pain or comfort. We are totally dependent on these giants and without them we would perish. Never again do we know the feeling of safeness that was ours in the warm, watery womb, and many of us spend years searching for that feeling again. We communicate with the giants by crying. But if we cry too much, the giants make unpleasant sounds and frightening faces. If we coo and smile, they give us love and sweet sounds back.

In time we identify the giants as Mommy and Daddy and come to accept them as the final authorities on everything. They encourage this and even demand it. How we interact emotionally with them seems to depend largely on them. Their responses to us appear to depend to a great extent on what they learned from their parents, modified by later learning. These early years are the beginning of our emotional-behavioral composite, our personalities. What we do and show, how we behave and reveal our feelings, seem to have only two alternatives—our way or our parents' way. Parents' ways usually prevail or appear to prevail. What we feel inside and may be hiding is also playing a major part in shaping us emotionally. Therein—deep inside us—troubles may begin to accumulate. Even while this relationship to our parents starts happening and shaping us, we meet the other major sphere of influence in our lives: We start school where we first meet our peers in strength.

PEERS

Now we find either a new problem or a new friendly power in the form of other little dominated people like ourselves. They make new and different demands on us. Sometimes their demands contradict our parents' demands. They may also contradict the exactions of the schoolteacher, the new additional authority figure in our lives. Soon we discover that sometimes when we do what our parents and the teacher tell us, the other little people disapprove. They point fingers accusing us of alienating ourselves from them, or trying to be teacher's pet. We *feel* their disapproval and it hurts.

How we interact with our peers and how we balance between them and authority figures begin to modify and change us. The interacting and the balancing add to and take from how we develop our emotional identity. I believe these feelings of inferiority last into adulthood for a majority. Maybe they last longer with alcoholics or persons with emotional problems. But I believe they last longer with most people than they are willing to admit.

Emotional maturity is achieved when we come to feel our own worthiness, a comfortable place among our peers, and an appropriate relationship to authority figures. I believe that to achieve a balance between the responses we give to authority figures and peers is one key to emotional health.

You, as a concerned person, for instance, cannot totally ignore the opinion and the pressures of your peers in trying to implement guided intervention. You must weigh the alternatives. The knowledge and experience of the guided intervention concept comes from an authority figure. One reason I have called it a love cure is to recognize the great power of peer influence. In popular terms *love* is seen as a legitimate reason for doing many things that might otherwise be unacceptable. Your peers will accept this. Therefore, we have used *love* as a second way of explaining behavior that might be questioned by your peers. Guided intervention *is* a *love* cure.

Why some people become alcoholics and some do not—even with similar backgrounds and drinking experiences—is still not known. About this there is little disagreement among alcohologists. Still much has been written about "the alcoholic personality."* One psychologist has attempted to

**The Personality of the Alcoholic, Guises of Dependency* by Howard T. Blane, Harper & Row, New York.

demonstrate that alcoholics seem to have in common a problem coping with their dependency needs, saying they are either overly dependent and dislike themselves for it, or they are afraid to show dependency on anyone, or they tend to swing from being overly dependent to being unrealistically independent. Isn't the problem a lack of balance between peers and authority? Overbalance in favor of authority figures or in favor of peers is too much dependence; exaggerated refusal of all responsiveness to peers or to authority figures is too much independence. The swinging problem is a manifestation of the conflict between peers and authority spheres of influence. I do not see this as exclusively related to the developing alcoholism.

Some writers have tried to make much over the sexual identification problems of the alcoholic, particularly the male. I don't believe it. Outside of the fact that people who drink excessively lose their sexual potency temporarily—until drinking stops—and that this is further complicated with repeated experiences of failure and frustration between lovers, I believe the sexual problems of alcoholics are little different from those of total abstainers.

Most experienced alcoholism counselors have discarded the notion espoused by some psychiatrists that alcoholism is merely the symptom of an underlying emotional disorder. While these psychiatrists are busy looking for the underlying emotional disorder, the alcoholic is busy planning his next drunk and fails to keep appointments. The result is that none of his problems get help.

THE PERSONALITY TYPES

Another help to understanding human behavior and alcohol-related behavior is to learn something about personality problems. For my purposes I have simplified and given familiar names to the traditional personality disorders as they are classified in psychiatry.* I have found that almost all my

**Outline of Psychiatry* by Leonard Cammer, McGraw-Hill, New York.

friends, members of my family, and others tend toward one of the disorders for which psychiatry has such foreboding names as "paranoid" and "sociopathic." By recognizing these personality tendencies in ourselves I believe we can come to better understand ourselves as well as our alcoholics. A word of caution, however. Just as labeling a person "alcoholic" can predispose him to justify further drinking "because I am an alcoholic," these labels should be used with the understanding that our goal is *to minimize the traits* that tend to place us in any group. *To rid ourselves of the identifying characteristic* should be the goal of identifying ourselves, not a rationale for *not* changing. Sometimes to tell a man that he is a freak is to make him want never to be a human being again. This must be avoided.

It has been helpful to me—particularly in some categories—to let alcoholics classify themselves. I particularly found it helpful in the case of what I call "fun heads." That was the category of my son, Charlie. When I told him that he was a fun head, he said, "Why didn't somebody tell me that before? That description [the symptoms were listed on a wall chart] fits me all the way." Seeing his problem identified in clinical terms without moralist denunciations helped him to accept himself and to do something about it.

Here are the problem personalities I found among alcoholics and others and my names for them. Find yourself and your alcoholic—or your tendencies and his tendencies—here and you will know yourself and your alcoholic a little better. Then work on what you have learned!

The Fumbler. This is a person who never learns to cope even with life's problems, large or small. His life is full of wrong decisions and he is easily influenced by both his peers and by authority figures. He frequently gets into serious problems as a result. The incidence of alcoholism runs high for these persons but I have found that when they can be brought under the influence of a secure and balanced environment, the alcoholism can be brought under control.

The Lonely Dreamer. This is the person who shys away from others and wants to be left alone. He appears timid and quiet and is addicted to daydreaming. He finds it hard to express gratitude or other emotions to anyone. His daydreaming can become total withdrawal from the real world around him. Dreamers can be helped in group therapy by slow empathetic breaking down of their fears and anxieties and helping them to acknowledge the group's acceptance. Many of them fail in AA because of their timidity and tendency to avoid crowds. But an understanding and patient sponsor and spouse can overcome their reluctance to accept AA.

The Mood Swinger. This is a person who is usually popular and well liked because of his outgoing way with people. He is gregarious, optimistic, and most pleasant and agreeable when he is in his "up" mood. His problem is mood swings. Without warning he will go into depressions, sometimes so deep as to make him prone to suicide. To help the mood swinger we must catch him in his depressed state—when he is much like a dreamer—and deal with his problem then. The trouble is mood swingers avoid coming in contact with everyone when they get into their low mood, frequently shutting themselves up behind closed doors. When they are alcoholics, their mood swings become exaggerated and their depressions more dangerous.

The Grouch. This person is the most difficult to reach effectively, especially until he had been correctly identified. A grouch is suspicious and untrusting of almost everyone. He is afraid to let others know the smallest unpleasant fact about himself because he feels he must be perfect before he can be accepted by the rest of humankind. He blames others for everything that happens to him. Persons who have had to start working at jobs usually reserved to adults while they were in their teens frequently become grouches. The adolescent years—roughly from thirteen to nineteen—mark the period when peer influence is at its peak. During these years we learn to trust or to distrust our peers. If we are associating with older people while working, we are not going to win the acceptance we would if we were associating with our own age group. It follows that the teen-age school dropout forced to work with older people is alienated from his own age group and becomes distrustful of them. A person who distrusts his peers is likely to become a grouch. Alcoholism sits hard on the grouch because he is convinced that to admit it is to admit that he is weak, immoral, untrustworthy, and unworthy. He is difficult to reach both in group therapy and AA meetings. But since he tends to trust authority figures he responds well in one-to-one counseling at the start.

The Cry Baby. This is a person whose answer to problems is to scream, cry, walk out of the room, throw a tantrum, or behave in some other childish way. He never bottles up any emotion. When he is glad he becomes the center of attention with his joy; when he is mad or sad, once again he demands everyone's attention. Failing to get it he will go to almost any extreme to make others acknowledge him, even if his conduct might be considered infantile. He is always quick to cry or to walk out of a room or to make a scene when other methods fail to get attention.

The Rigid Preacher. This is the person who has adopted without question a strict code of conduct for himself from which he will not deviate and which he tries with fanatical determination to thrust on others. He drives himself unrelentingly until he lives in a state of tension and rigidity that makes him more talking machine than human. This is an uncommon personality problem for alcoholics.

The Fun Head. Variations of this makes up the most common personality problem (or character defect) among alcoholics. The fun head is the opposite of the rigid preacher. He knows no code of conduct except that of his own pleasure and his own desires. He follows no rule of conduct except that of self-gratification. He cannot tolerate pain or any discomfort for any length of time. He will avoid waiting for a simple pleasure if there is any way to do it. He lives by the pleasure principle. If it's fun, he's for it; if it's not fun, he's against it! He will invariably take advantage of the kindness of others. Sometimes he is like the mood swinger in his ability to get along with others, but he leaves friendships behind as soon as it serves his purpose to take up with something or someone new. He never does anything for others unless there is an immediate reward. He is the complete optimist, always believing there will be a pot of gold at the end of the rainbow and that the most vexing problem will resolve itself without any sacrifice for him. The fun head is a con man, learning how to get others to do his work, run his errands, keep him supplied with his needs regardless of how deprived others might be around him.

I have found that fun heads can be reasonable and can be helped once the self-destructiveness of their way of living can be demonstrated to them. They sometimes have identical tastes, dress, and attitudes of teen-agers who have never accepted responsibility. Frequently they carry even the physical youthful appearance of adolescents into their forties. They particularly do not understand or accept social responsibility. When these things can be demonstrated to them in tangible terms, progress can be made. The problem is to be able to keep in contact with them long enough to do the job. I believe the fun head who becomes an alcoholic and who seeks help is one of the most promising candidates for the techniques of guided intervention.

At one time psychiatry classified all alcoholics as persons with "sociopathic personality disturbances" or what I call the fun head syndrome. It has been established that many other personality types become alcoholic and that some are one hundred and eighty degrees removed from these behavioral problems.

Concerned persons of alcoholics can, with the help of their counselors, understand their alcoholics better by determining into which behavioral classification they fit. If your alcoholic is more fun head than grouch, then you can and should be very strict and demanding with him. If you are certain he is a fun head, his threats of suicide, for example, can usually be taken as another con, a means of winning his way. Few fun heads take their own lives. But if he is a mood swinger, is happy, then suddenly has depressed manifestations, his talk of suicide needs to be considered more seriously when he is in a depression. The daydreaming habit of the dreamers may rescue him from his loneliness and may save him from taking the ultimate way out by suicide. But the sudden depression of the mood swinger—with or without alcohol—is dangerous. Fun heads, after learning the description of a mood swinger, like to take that category for themselves. Fun heads are always prone to fool us. Just remember, the true mood swinger expresses more joie de vivre when he is in his "up" swing while the fun head is usually never quite satisfied, asking for just a little more. The mood swinger gets into a genuine deep depression. He won't talk and he gets away from people in unmistakable ways. He is difficult to find when he wants to hide. The fun head simply gets bored and complains. His depressions are greatly exaggerated and don't last long.

If you determine that your alcoholic has the characteristics of the grouch, then remember that he may find it harder to be convinced that you love him when you use guided intervention. Your moves for increasing pressures need to be applied with more patience and longer waiting periods than with a fun head.

Personality problems are related to how we respond to authority figures and to our peers. For mental health we need to take into consideration authority figures for their knowledge and experience without letting these considerations preclude informal and social relationships. We need to accept and be accepted by our peers without giving way to perpetual social adolescence. If authority figures are accepted to the exclusion of our peers, we may become grouches and preachers. If we cater exclusively to peer influence as teen-agers tend to, we become irresponsible fun heads. Mental health centers are overcrowded with the grouches and dreamers who got that way from overresponding to authority figures. Many grouches and dreamers become alcoholics when they experience the relief from tension and the demands they make on themselves that alcohol can bring. For a fun head alcohol comes as just another pleasure he feels is his due. It is easy for the fun head to get into the clutches of alcohol addiction if he gets into the habit of indulging himself and avoiding sacrifice, pain, and discomfort.

Once a person becomes an alcohol addict, alcoholism becomes the number one problem in his life. Contrary to some psychotherapists, alcoholism is a basic and primary condition that must take precedence over other illnesses. To treat another illness while ignoring the presence of alcoholism may mean to deny the patient all help. Drinking behavior prevents the delivery of almost every medical or psychiatric treatment to its effective conclusion. That is why alcoholism requires primary consideration. Other ailments can be treated simultaneously but the presence of alcoholism must be recognized and acknowledged.

Determining anyone's personality disorder will neither resolve that problem nor his alcoholism. Neither does it excuse his behavior or yours. We humans are highly individualistic and frequently unpredictable.

My purpose has been to help you understand your own behavioral tendencies as well as your alcoholic's. If the fun head shoe or the grouch shoe fits, for heaven's sake, *don't wear it!* Get a new shoe, get a prettier and healthier shoe. Seek to be wiser—not cynical—in understanding your alcoholic and yourself. Don't accept his behavior as final but be understanding and accepting of him as a troubled person. Give him mature love and firm support.

PARENT, ADULT, AND CHILD

One of the best aids I have ever found to overcoming the problems of human communication is Eric Berne's Transactional Analysis.* We recommend to our clients at Azalea Center the easier-to-read book *I'm OK—You're OK* by Thomas A. Harris. This book has nothing to do with alcoholism, but the first six chapters especially give a lucid explanation of why we have problems communicating with one another and open the way to finding solutions.

Transactional analysis (often called TA) has become an almost universal reference tool for American psychotherapists. It gives an ongoing second-by-second understanding of what is happening inside a human being as opposed to the "frozen" personality classifications that I borrowed from psychiatry. Psychiatry classifies the patterns of behavior that I have given the names of "grouch," "fun head," and so forth. Transactional analysis examines the emotion at the moment of communication. We learn how to ask and to answer the questions: Who is the sender? Who is the receiver?

**Transactional Analysis in Psychotherapy: A Systematic Individual and Social Psychiatry* by Eric Berne, M.D., Grove Press, Inc., New York.

Each signal is called a transaction, a communication between humans, one to one or one to several. Transactional analysis consists of analyzing these transactions in preconceived terms or ego states. The key terms in TA are parent, adult, and child. These three words are given special definitions. It is important to understand them.

The late Dr. Berne, a California psychiatrist and author of the best seller *Games People Play* discovered his system while counseling an attorney. The lawyer told him one day that when he came to see Berne he felt like a child and not like the respected member of the bar he knew he was. Berne began to notice that the attorney was not the only one of his patients who actually changed personality while in a therapeutic visit with him. He came to see that all persons seemed to have three distinct identities into which they put themselves at various times. He called them child, parent, and adult.

A person is "in his child" when he is reacting with raw or unrestrained emotion or when he is taking a childlike attitude in a transaction with another person.

A person is "in his parent" when he is reacting in ways learned from others by imitating them, repeating their ideas. He is also in his parent when he attempts to impose his ideas onto someone else or assumes the attitude of a parent or teacher.

A person is "in his adult" when he is using all his faculties to act or react in the most reasonable and appropriate possible way.

One way to get the child, parent, and adult concepts in mind is to remember their prototypes. The prototype of the child is the clown, always either laughing or crying. Or, it might be the legendary prostitute with a heart of gold who doesn't mean any harm but who supposedly makes a career of raw emotional pleasures without taking into consideration the consequences.

The prototype of the parent is the Bible-quoting minister who refuses to reason or explain but who answers every problem and every question with a biblical quotation, whether appropriate or not. Obviously, the parent's prototype is also the real-life parents who answer their children's questioning of why they must go to bed early with the dogmatic, "Because Mommy says so."

Another almost equally useful tool of TA is the concept of "games" and "game playing." Most methods of solving problems and responding to others among immature or neurotic persons fall into neatly fitting interacting patterns. TA has categorized almost all conceivable interactions and given them names. These, too, have gained wide usage among American psychotherapists.

Transactional analysis has given birth to many books and monograms. One of the many uses it affords is a system of analyzing what happens when two people exchange messages. An example is when a person in his parent addresses the child in another person and that person responds from his own parent and addresses the first person's child. This becomes a "crossed transaction" that results in unpleasantness and thus blocks effective communication. Why and how this happens can be charted on paper with a minimum of practice and can improve one's own communications with others, particularly between husbands and wives. In TA terms the fun head is a person who tries to stay in his child most of the time. Likewise, a drunk might be a person escaping into his child because he cannot relax and get into it while he is sober. The grouch may be frequently locked in his parent and cannot release himself. The grouch might get drunk to free himself from the self-imposed bonds of his parent.

Getting into our adult—although not to stay there permanently—can be described as the goal of most therapy. But for some of us, learning to get into our child can be as important to survival as to find our adult. The adult of TA is the identity we assume when we run a problem through our child for emotional content, through our parent for what we may have been taught or previously experienced about it, and come out with the most intelligent and appropriate result. Consider an opera singer. Singing without training may be enjoyable fun and gives anyone good emotional release (child). But when a trained operatic tenor sings he is combining emotion and feeling (child) with years and years of discipline and training (parent) to give us a beautiful and inspiring (adult) result.

If you are a concerned person, you may improve your communication with your alcoholic by becoming familiar with the parent, adult, and child identities of transactional analysis, which you can learn from one of several books on the subject. You may also get to understand him better by coming to understand him as a fumbler, a dreamer, a mood swinger, a grouch, a cry baby, a rigid preacher, or a fun head. But these are preliminary concepts. Now let us focus on alcoholism itself.

FEELING GRAPH

To understand your alcoholic best of all, I urge you to read *I'll Quit Tomorrow* by Vernon E. Johnson. I shall attempt to encapsulate Johnson's excellent explanation of what happens to an individual who becomes an alcoholic. We have used it for several years at Samaritan Center and Azalea Center after receiving two visits from Vern Johnson (his doctorate is in divinity and he is an Episcopal priest) before his book was published.

Johnson draws a horizontal line that he calls a "feeling graph," labeling one end "euphoria" and the other "depression" or "pain." In our variation we draw the line vertically, the high end being euphoria and the bottom extremity, depression. The very top of the line represents the highest feeling of joy a person can experience and the bottom place on the line the lowest depression. A "normal" person finds himself squarely in the middle. Exactly in the center of the line we mark off a section labeled "normal." The bottom and top of this middle marked-off section designate the upper and lower boundaries of "normal." When a "normal" person has a drink of an alcoholic beverage, his "feeling" moves up toward euphoria. He feels happy. But he stays within the normal limits. If he has two drinks, he moves up a little higher. When the effect of the alcohol wears off, his emotions return to the center, the normal middle position. If he has not overindulged, theoretically, no harm has been done and he is back where he started.

But a person who is becoming an alcohol addict repeats this experience. Over and over. He not only likes the feeling, but he also wants to feel it again and again. After a while he begins to move up above the boundaries of "normal," getting nearer the top marked euphoria. Getting drunk and too "happy" also causes him to get silly, irresponsible, and frequently so uninhibited as to do things that cause problems and get him into trouble. Each time he has this kind of experience—overindulging and doing things he wishes later he had not done—he has an unpleasant result when he sobers up. Instead of ending up within the normal boundaries where he supposedly started, the person becoming an alcoholic starts ending up on the lower side of normal. The first few times he is only a little depressed and sad over the results and not quite below the boundary of normal limits. But finally he begins to end every drunken episode below the normal section of the feeling graph. This is easy to understand considering the fact that he is being told by his wife and others that he made a fool of himself. Or, perhaps he has experienced his first arrest for drunkenness or drunk driving.

The alcoholism begins to progress to the point where the victim begins to stay on the depressed side of the normal limits. He lives there. He stays sad. He stays depressed. He begins to hate himself, especially when he realizes that no matter how many times he promises himself or his wife or his boss that he will never do it again, he goes back and does the same thing again and again and again.

This is the story of alcoholism. This is the alcoholic. He is a depressed, sad, and frightened person who discovers he has come up against a force he cannot control. He discovers that no matter how simple it may seem to others, he cannot successfully make it through a given period without his booze.

Finally, he reaches the stage where he lives under the normal side of the feeling graph, in the depressed area, and he discovers he never makes it up to the happy euphoric side again no matter how much he drinks. In fact, he discovers he has to drink just to get into the normal area, just to feel adequate or "normal."

This is the picture of alcoholism in agreement with my

observations and experiences over the past twelve years with some 1,300 alcoholics. I have read other intricate explanations of alcoholic personalities and conflicts. One pictures the victim as an angry person, turning the anger against himself and others. But I have not seen nearly as many alcoholics angry as I have seen them sad and depressed. Hating themselves. I have seen them resigned to their fate, which they see as a lifelong unquenchable thirst for more and more alcohol. I believe almost every alcoholic I have known disliked himself. That is my definition of depression. That is also the alcoholic's home.

DEFENSE MECHANISMS

What happens to a person who hates himself so? What happens to the alcoholic who makes this discovery about himself, about his total dependency on alcohol? One thing that happens frequently is that he kills himself. One statistic* says that 31 percent of all suicides in the United States are by alcoholics. Self-destruction is the logical end for a person who gets into a depressed state and cannot extricate himself. But all alcoholics do not take their own lives the quick way. Most of them do it in slow motion.

The human mind and emotional system is a marvelous thing to behold. It has devices to take care of problems. Sometimes these devices complicate the problem when used excessively. But other times they save the user from himself when the truth is too bitter to accept. These devices are called defense mechanisms, a kind of moving, dynamic system that filters and screens the truth. The indigestible truths are kept out; the others come through distorted and disguised so that an unreal world is seen by the user.

There are many defense mechanisms but it is sufficient here to deal with three. The first is *denial.* Propagandists know that if a lie is repeated often enough people can be made to believe it. This is even more true of one person in

**Frontiers of Alcoholism* by Morris E. Chafetz, Science House, New York.

relation to himself. When an alcoholic (or any person) faces a truth too terrible to bear, he can simply *deny* it to himself. It just isn't so, he tells himself, over and over. If he does it enough, he can convince himself. Soon he believes it, at least long enough to be able to deny it to other people.

The second defense mechanism is *rationalization,* or phony reasoning. The alcoholic hears himself described as an alcoholic because of his regular and repeated drunken episodes. But because he has never lost a day of work or actually taken a drink "on the job"—although he may be drinking within minutes of leaving work—he convinces himself that his actions are not "alcoholism." He *rationalizes* away the fear that he is an alcoholic.

The least familiar defense mechanism is the third—*projection.* This is attributing to others faults or weaknesses we see in ourselves and cannot allow ourselves to identify as our own. So we attribute them to some other person. An alcoholic begins to suspect he drinks too much for obvious reasons. But instead of looking at his drinking, he might project by noticing every drink his wife has. He dwells on this constantly and thus avoids looking at himself.

Another way to project is to find fault with other people so that there isn't time to look at ourselves. Many middle-age Americans today are decrying the terrible drug habits of the new generation while they themselves get drunk on alcohol regularly and think nothing of it.

Such is the psychological picture of almost every alcoholic. No matter how little or how much education, money, position, and achievement he has, this system of defenses keeps him from accepting his problem. To accept it is to accept depression, an intolerable state of being, one that no human can long endure. To understand the alcoholic's dilemma, we must know that when we take away his alcohol and also take away his defense mechanisms, we had better have something to put in their place. We must replace the alcohol and we must find a way to make the defense mechanisms no longer necessary.

In guided intervention we attack the defense mechanisms with gentle suggestions at first. We apply pressures with care and forethought like surgical knives cutting at the defenses but providing understanding at the same time. By sending the alcoholic to AA, group therapy, or counseling, we catch him as he gives up both alcohol and his defense mechanisms. We hope he will start liking himself and, with the help of other alcoholics or a therapist, will build up strength to live without chemical crutches and eventually have little need for denying, rationalizing, and projecting.

There are two other mechanisms that go with the alcoholic person. One is the phenomenon of blacking out. This is the memory lapse that seems to go with heavy drinking for most alcoholics. After a few drinks he is unable to remember anything that happens. This seems to be one of nature's additional ways of protecting him against himself, a sort of physical defense mechanism, temporary amnesia. Blacking out is rarely understood by nonalcoholics. Even the alcoholic is frequently unaware of its pervasiveness. He cannot believe the terrible tales he hears about himself since he has no memory of them. So he may attribute them to exaggerations and hostility. The nonalcoholic meanwhile cannot believe that the alcoholic (who is remembered as having been "wide awake") cannot remember something as terrible and real as the drunken conduct that caused much distress when it happened.

The other mark of the alcoholic that I have observed is what Johnson calls "euphoric recall." This is the ability of the alcoholic to remember every pleasant thing about drinking that happens to him and a remarkable *inability* to recall any unpleasant experience connected with his drinking. Johnson calls it a "built-in" blackout system.

You, the concerned person, seeking to understand the conduct of an alcoholic, might do well to mark the five characteristics on the fingers of one hand. The three defense mechanisms that every alcoholic uses: one, *denial;* two, *rationalization;* three, *projection.* Then, add to these the two *blackout systems,* the temporary amnesia most alcoholics experience and the "built-in" blackout system with which he recalls how happy the drinking experiences were and forgets how unpleasant and tragic were the consequences.

I particularly commend these five characteristics to concerned persons because I have found that many of you are prone to reinforcing them in your alcoholics. And in so doing you frequently become co-victims of the problem. Here is what Dr. Karl Menninger wrote in 1938 about all concerned persons of alcoholics:*

"I must mention another curious but almost invariable phenomenon in alcoholism cases. This is the characteristic pathological optimism from which both the alcoholic patient and all members of his family seem regularly to suffer. The word 'suffer' is chosen advisedly because as a rule this attitude is the most serious obstacle to the successful treatment of the affliction. No matter how desperate the case may seem at first or how dismal or tragic the history, it is usually only a matter of a few weeks or months until the patient and (what is really much more strange) his relatives are convinced that he is now perfectly well, has made a radical change in his psychology, will never fall into such a habit again, and should accordingly be trusted and expected to resume his full share of responsibilities in his life. Even when this same trick, this same formula or promise and disappointment, has been repeated over and over, it still works because the members of the family want to believe it. It is the vicious circle of interaction between the mutual agressions of patient and family."

To summarize: Science has not found the basic cause of alcoholism, but most experts agree it is partly physical, partly psychological, and partly sociological. To understand an alcoholic person you should understand human emotional development and personality disorders. Once a person becomes a chronic alcoholic, certain recognizable patterns of attitude and behavior take place. He becomes deeply depressed, i.e., he dislikes or even hates himself. Unable to survive with self-hate, he develops a system of defenses including denial, rationalization, and preoccupation with other people's problems. He resists penetration of these defenses so staunchly that only experienced and knowledgeable specialists can tear them down. The goal of alcoholism therapy is to penetrate these defenses and rescue the alcoholic from his delusions while restoring self-esteem and love.

**Man Against Himself* by Karl Menninger, Harcourt, Brace and World, Inc., New York.

10

Where Alcoholics Learn to Stop Drinking

The most successful treatment methods for alcoholics seem to have two things in common. They confront the victim with the fact of his illness, and they do it constructively. The third necessary ingredient may not always be included as an integral part of the treatment, but it should be. That is, that it should be a continuing process of at least two years during which the alcoholic is being confronted constructively. The three together are *continuing constructive confrontation.* The three Cs. Finally, to succeed, every alcoholic should receive another ingredient. It may vary from one case to another. But there must be something—a great love, a revitalized marriage, a new reason to live, a religious conversion, or another new interest or pleasure in life to fill the void left by removing the alcohol. If this fourth ingredient is missing, the alcoholic is likely to return to drinking sooner or later. But with all *four* ingredients, permanent sobriety is almost guaranteed.

The two most familiar alcoholism therapies in the United States are Alcoholics Anonymous and what is called encounter group therapy.

AA is available free at any of thousands of autonomous groups meeting weekly in the United States and the world. Group therapy for alcoholics is offered by several hundred rehabilitation and treatment centers on both an inpatient and outpatient basis. Most of these either employ AA orientation or include it.

But you can never afford to overlook this truth: The professionally oriented group therapies will be effective for your alcoholic initially only if they enable him to accept his problem. If the therapist or group leader does not understand the quintessence of the *primary* nature of alcoholism or if the therapist does not know he is dealing with an alcoholic and what that means, the treatment is doomed to failure. Your alcoholic can be taught or "facilitated" to change his life habits, understand his underlying emotional problems and how to deal with them, and even to change some of his personality traits and attitudes, and still continue or return to drinking. If he has not been confronted and accepted the basic fact of his alcoholism, all the psychotherapy in the world will not bring about a lasting change in his drinking. It is not even particularly helpful to analyze the reasons that led to a drinking episode. I am convinced that a majority of drinking interruptions by alcoholics who are being monitored in a treatment program occur simply because they are alcohol addicts. Most drinking episodes occur in cycles. When an alcoholic has gone into treatment and seems to be making progress and then has an interruption of sobriety, I believe it is because his drinking cycle has come full circle and caught him and his counselors unaware. It is helpful to establish your alcoholic's drinking cycle and to be especially watchful when it comes around. No one may be able to prevent it but at least you might try at the right time. And frequently an alcoholic will almost unconsciously ask for help when he feels it coming. However, remember *you cannot stop him from drinking. Only he can stop himself.*

Alcoholics are often encouraged by their therapists to look for the "reason" for the drinking episode. This is really of dubious help. Sooner or later the alcoholic would have gotten drunk anyway unless an alert vigilance had been kept by the alcoholic himself, with or without the help of others. It isn't why the alcoholic *started* drinking that matters, but rather why he did not *stop* himself from drinking. The more positive therapeutic helps won't matter until a long period of sobriety has been experienced. In the early period of any program it is a question of *stopping* or *preventing* the anticipatory moves that lead up to the drink and stopping the final act itself. It is not a question of what *started* the events in the first place. The urge to drink lies kicking and screaming deep within the alcoholic even when he believes and to all appearances acts as if it is dormant. The safest assumption to make in the case of every chronic alcoholic is that *he is going to drink* at some time or another unless he *stops himself.* He is always just a "drink away from a drunk" and less than *minutes* away from a drink in the early stages of any program. He will continue to be that way for a long time. This is why regular continuous confrontation is essential to successful treatment. Now let us look at how constructive confrontation is built into the AA program.

THE FIRST AA MEETING

AA is the most continuous confrontive therapy offered to alcoholics. From the minute the alcoholic walks into an AA meeting or even a meeting room (if it is not the day or time for a meeting) he is being confronted. It may be a mild confrontation and it may be indirect.

Let's say that your husband or wife is the alcoholic being taken into an AA meeting for the first time by another AA member. The scene might be like this:

Old Member (just before entering the room with your

alcoholic): "Relax now, everything is going to be all right." (But he is thinking: You are going to meet some live admitted alcoholics. They are going to welcome you even though they are going to look at you as an alcoholic too, even though you haven't admitted you are one.)

The confrontation has begun—unnamed, unadmitted, and even denied by all—because the visiting potential member knows correctly that everyone is going to assume he is an alcoholic.

Your Alcoholic (trying to appear unconcerned): "Oh sure, I understand. Don't worry about me." (But he is thinking: I can take it. So they think I am an alcoholic. I know I'm not. Let them think anything they want. I can show them if I have to!)

Old Member (meeting another old member): "Hey, Joe. I want you to meet a friend of mine. He's attending his first meeting. Wants to look us over." (Meaning: Here's one of those people who cannot admit anything. Be careful what you say. Don't run him off. Remember your own first meeting!)

Old Member Joe (smiling and offering his hand for a shake): "Hello. I'm glad to meet you. Say, would you like a cup of coffee?" (Being protective, he doesn't ask the new person's name and he hasn't been told the name.)

From that point on the conversation could be about anything—weather, sports, world happenings, or anything unrelated to drinking, alcohol, alcoholics, why your alcoholic is there, or why anyone else is there. But the confrontive experience is being felt nonetheless. Your alcoholic *knows* why he is there and he knows why everyone else is there and he cannot think of anything else unless it might be his strong desire to get out or to get a drink or both.

A few minutes later the meeting begins. AA meetings follow a familiar ritual. The chairman or the secretary (usually serving a month at a time) opens the meeting, calling for a moment of silent prayer. Then he says:

"Hello. My name is Max H." Or frequently these days he gives his full name. "I am an alcoholic." (This phrase is a must; it is rarely if ever omitted so that the alcoholic is, in fact, confronting himself, reminding himself.) "But by the grace of God and the help of AA and many people like you out there, I am here and sober tonight.

"This is the regular Monday night meeting of the East City Group of Alcoholics Anonymous.

"Alcoholics Anonymous is an informal society of alcoholics whose aim is to help fellow problem drinkers recover their health. We know many of our members have already laid their foundation for permanent recovery in spite of the fact that we have often been pronounced incurable."

This written message is read at the beginning of almost every AA meeting. It begins and ends speaking to the problem of alcoholism to the exclusion of anything else. It continues:

"Not being reformers, we offer our help and experience only to those who want it."

With these words the members of AA inform your alcoholic that he must assume responsibility for his own problem. If he wants help, it is there. But "only to those who want it." The reading continues:

"We alcoholics are gathered together seeking a renewal of strength. This strength has been revealed to us as coming from a Power higher than any earthly one. However, we foster no particular creed or sect nor do we oppose anyone."

Alcoholics Anonymous has a unique take-it-or-leave-it spiritual side that eventually most successful members accept. Some of the most moving spiritual testimonies I have ever heard, in or out of church, were made in AA meetings. Next the reading returns to the meaning of membership:

"The only requirement for membership is a desire to stop drinking."

This statement may vary from group to group. Sometimes it reads: "The only requirement for membership is an *honest* desire . . . " or "an honest willingness to do anything to stop drinking." All three phrases may be found in AA literature, but the "Big Book" of AA, the basic text from which the fellowship derives its name *Alcoholics Anonymous,** states as the third tradition of AA, "the only requirement for AA

**Alcoholics Anonymous,* Alcoholics Anonymous World Services, Inc., New York City.

membership is a desire to stop drinking." The reading continues:

"Each person present is requested to observe the exact meaning of the word anonymous as many of our members wish to remain anonymous."

Here your alcoholic is reassured that his presence at the meeting is not supposed to be reported outside the occasion. This is of inestimable help in the early period of recovery for the alcoholic frightened at the prospect of being branded "alcoholic."

"Each speaker on our program presents his or her own views and experiences. His or her opinions are not necessarily those of the group as a whole."

The speaker, who may have been the secretary, then usually turns the program over to the chairman.

The chairman repeats the ritual of self-confrontation. "Hello. My name is James S. I am an alcoholic. But through the help of a power greater than myself, that I choose to call God, I have not had a drink—or any mood-altering drug—since October 7, 1970. I am grateful to Alcoholics Anonymous and people like you here tonight for my sobriety. I have asked Charlie P. to read 'How It Works' from chapter 5 of the 'Big Book.' "

Then Charlie P. might reply, saying:

"My name is Charlie P. and I, too, am an alcoholic. But through the help of AA and people like all of you here—and a lot of work on my part and many prayers—I am here and sober tonight. And for that I am most grateful. I will now read 'How It Works.'

"Rarely have we seen a person fail who has thoroughly followed our path. Those who do not recover are people who cannot or will not completely give themselves to this simple program, usually men and women who are constitutionally incapable of being honest with themselves. There are such unfortunates. They are not at fault; they seem to have been born that way. They are naturally incapable of grasping and developing a manner of living that demands rigorous honesty. Their chances are less than average. There are those, too, who suffer from grave emotional and mental disorders, but many of them do recover if they have the capacity to be honest."

These words from the AA book inform your alcoholic that he can recover if he can be honest with himself. In fact, they tell him that "rigorous honesty" is called for. It also refers to the AA program as a simple one and holds out hope to the visiting potential member.

Over and over at this point the visitor is being confronted with the facts about alcoholism and about AA. There is no place for him to turn. No one is speaking directly to him. Yet, your alcoholic knows the message is really for him if he is listening!

Charlie P. continues reading from chapter 5:

"Our stories disclose in a general way what we used to be like, what happened, and what we are like now."

This sentence has been taken to be almost a direction by many AA members as to what their testimony should cover when they speak, i.e., "what it used to be like, what happened, and what it is like now."

"If you have decided you want what we have and are willing to go to any length to get it, then you are ready to take certain steps."

There is to follow in a moment the reading of the AA's Twelve *Suggested* Steps. But notice the buildup and elaborate introduction they receive.

"At some of these we balked. We thought we could find an easier, softer way. But we could not. With all the *earnestness at our command, we beg of you to be fearless and thorough* from the very start. Some of us have tried to hold on to our old ideas and the result was nil until we let go absolutely."

Here your alcoholic is being implored to join the great fellowship, to "let go absolutely." Charlie P. continues:

"Remember that we deal with alcohol—*cunning, baffling, powerful!* Without help *it is too much for us.* But there is One who has all power—that One is God. *May you find Him now!*"

Once again the visitor is being urged with unequivocable language. If he is listening, your alcoholic may be moved as he has never been moved before.

"Half measures availed us nothing. We stood at the turning point. We asked His protection and care with *complete abandon.*"

THE TWELVE STEPS

Here are the steps we took, which are suggested as a program of recovery:

1. We admitted we were powerless over alcohol—that our lives had become unmanageable.
2. Came to believe that a Power greater than ourselves could restore us to sanity.
3. Made a decision to turn our will and our lives over to the care of God *as we understood Him.*
4. Made a searching and fearless moral inventory of ourselves.
5. Admitted to God, to ourselves, and to another human being the exact nature of our wrongs.
6. Were entirely ready to have God remove all these defects of character.
7. Humbly asked Him to remove our shortcomings.
8. Made a list of all persons we had harmed, and became willing to make amends to them all.
9. Made direct amends to such people wherever possible, except when to do so would injure them or others.
10. Continued to take personal inventory and when we were wrong promptly admitted it.
11. Sought through prayer and meditation to improve our conscious contact with God *as we understood Him,* praying only for knowledge of His will for us and the power to carry that out.
12. Having had a spiritual awakening as the result of these steps, we tried to carry this message to alcoholics, and to practice these principles in all our affairs.

At this point, almost as if anticipating what your frightened visiting nonadmitted alcoholic might be saying to himself, the text reads:

"Many of us exclaimed, 'What an order! I can't go through with it.'

"Do not be discouraged. No one among us has been able to maintain anything like perfect adherence to these principles. We are not saints. The point is that we are willing to grow along spiritual lines. The principles we have set down are guides to progress. We claim spiritual progress rather than spiritual perfection.

"Our description of the alcoholic, the chapter on the agnostic, and our personal adventures before and after make clear three pertinent ideas:

"1. That we were alcoholic and could not manage our own lives.

"2. That probably no human power could have relieved our alcoholism.

"3. That God could and would if He were sought."

Following these preliminaries, the AA meeting then is taken over by the chairman. It may be a meeting featuring an accomplished AA veteran, a speaker with a moving story of "how it was, what happened, and what it is like now." It might feature two or three "birthdays," in which the speakers are observing the anniversary of a given number of years sobriety. Or it might be a discussion meeting in which the speaker introduces a topic and asks each member present to talk about it.

AA meetings are usually blessed with their informality. Most chairmen always leave time for a fellow member who may have a particular need to unburden himself of his own problem that night. Almost all AA meetings have the essential ingredients for recovery: continuing constructive confrontation. They are continuing confrontation because all AA meetings are about drinking, getting drunk, and finding recovery. The very ritualistic nature of the so-called drunkalogues and the reading of the Twelve Steps and "How It Works," along with repeated personal testimonies, never allows an alcoholic to forget why he is there and "how it was" before he stopped drinking. For alcoholics who might no longer have the continuing need for being so reminded—after years of successful sobriety—the benefits come from participation in the help for recovery offered to so many who do need it. Helping others (called Twelfth Step work in AA) provides the certain additional "something" for sustaining sobriety after a period of at least two years of active constructive confrontation.

Many theories are advanced to explain why AA works. Some members say that the most important thing to remember is to keep attending meetings. Yet, obviously, a person must participate in some way or start *identifying* with the other alcoholics to derive benefit. Others say, perhaps more often, that it is essential to "work" the Twelve Steps. But since there is no structured outline for checking on who takes them and who doesn't, it seems unlikely that all successful members go through them. As a matter of fact, when the discussion is on one of the steps, I have heard many old members acknowledge that they are "still working on that one" or "that's one I don't guess I'll ever do right."

The spiritual aspect of the steps seems to frighten some alcoholics who feel that they have drifted away from their childhood faith too far to ever be forgiven by their God. This is why the steps carefully couch the references to God with the phrase "as we understood Him." Some AA members go to the extreme of recommending to the newcomer that he use any Higher Power he choses, even inanimate objects. Although almost nonsensical, this advice to the newcomer seems to serve the purpose of totally removing the idea of God from any unpleasant childhood religious association that may have become a psychological threat to him.

Above all, AA gatherings and AA methods are pragmatic. "Use it if it works," is the advice frequently given. "Take it with you if it helps you. Leave it here if you don't like it" is another counsel one hears at AA.

But whatever happens, it is the continuing aspect that seems to be the most important. Forming enduring social relationships with other members, identifying with the speakers, and finding much in common with many eventually make the AA meeting a pleasant social, psychological, and spiritual experience.

The very fact that AA is *confrontive* is the most common excuse given by the newcomer for not attending. "I don't like to hear all those drunks' stories. I was never that bad. I don't see how that can help me. What I need to do is to find a new life and forget that." So goes the typical attack on AA by the unwilling problem drinker.

But the reason your alcoholic does not want to hear the drunkalogues is most likely because he finds himself identifying too much with the speaker. For many this is painfully embarrassing. Intolerable. I remember the first time it was explained to me. A middle-aged professional person of my acquaintance was explaining why some alcoholics would never attend AA.

"It's terrifying and threatening to them to hear themselves and see themselves stripped naked in front of all those people. It is simply too much for them to bear!" she said.

I was impressed. It had never been explained to me so clearly. Then several years later I was consulted by this woman's husband. She was an alcoholic herself! No wonder she understood the frightening aspect of AA testimonials! She understood how frightening the AA confrontation is (even though it is indirect) because she herself was experiencing it. She felt its force, its strength—the real pain of it—precisely because she was an alcoholic herself and would not accept it. Confrontation is painful and in extremely rare cases—such as a borderline schizophrenic person—it might be dangerous. (It might cause a so-called psychotic break.) But it is absolutely essential to recovery. Without coming to grips with this painful fact, an alcoholic has no real hope of lifetime recovery.

The answer to this problem—and it is a serious one—is for your alcoholic to have strong reinforcement while he is learning to face up to his problem. You, the concerned person, must bear this in mind. After you, the most important person is a good AA sponsor.

The sponsor's role in AA is sometimes overlooked. Although a few AA members may succeed without one, having a veteran AA member to call upon for help is almost indispensable. Your alcoholic should be encouraged to get a sponsor and to get a new one if the old sponsor fails to respond to his need.

My advice to any spouse of an alcoholic who starts going to AA is to go with him or make certain he has a sponsor who cares and who works at his assignment. Most important of all, you, the concerned person, should bear in mind: If your alcoholic continues to go to AA meetings with regularity—and starts and continues a period of uninterrupted sobriety that can be sustained for at least two years—permanent sobriety is likely.

If your alcoholic has started attending AA meetings and continues to get drunk or to have so-called slips on occasion, the prognosis is poor. You, the concerned person, must take due note of what is happening and take steps to increase the therapy.

If your alcoholic begins an AA program, the questions you should check on are these:

1. Is your alcoholic participating in a *feeling* way in the meetings? Does he or she ever speak? Does he seem to be talking honestly? Does he freely admit to his problem in his own words or is he just *parroting* other members' clichés?

2. Does he seem to *enjoy* going to the meetings or does he go because he is forced and coerced? Most alcoholics will eventually reach the stage in which they enjoy the meetings. Until he does, he needs to be either guided into continued attendance or guided into some other kind of therapy.

3. Does he have a sponsor who cares about what is happening to him? Does the sponsor regularly call on your alcoholic and inquire about him or her? If no active sponsor has been found, you should encourage your alcoholic to find another sponsor or to get one for the first time if none has been obtained.

4. Is your alcoholic trying to "work" the steps? If he or she makes no moves acknowledging the importance of the steps in at least a precursory fashion, you should encourage him to do something about them.

Obviously, if he never takes the first step—acknowledging his inability to handle alcohol and the unmanageability of his life with alcohol—he will never stop drinking. Frequently a good sponsor will confront the alcoholic with his evasiveness and call him or her to task for failure to take the first step. Making this admission is the indispensable step for successful recovery from alcohol addiction in *any* program.

If the answers to these four groups of questions are negative, then the problem with your alcoholic and his relationship to AA becomes obvious. You need to take every possible step to remedy the situation by whatever means are available, using the techniques of guided intervention. If your alcoholic continues to insist that AA will not work for him or her, then alternatives need to be offered.

Keep this in mind: In almost every instance the person rejecting AA after attending at least six or seven meetings will really be rejecting *any* serious attempt to help his problem. Do not accept the AA putdown too quickly.

If I were to give a short answer to the question raised in the title of this chapter, Where alcoholics learn to stop drinking, I would say "at meetings for alcoholics." As long as the meetings are good AA or good alcoholism therapy meetings with experienced people in the field and as long as going to meetings is continued with constructive confrontation, the results will be good. What are the basic differences in AA meetings and group therapy for alcoholics?

The basic differences between alcoholism group therapy and AA is that AA starts with more leeway for the alcoholic and ends up with more structure. In the beginning of AA your alcoholic sets his own pace. He may be allowed to go for weeks or months and even years before acknowledging himself as an alcoholic. But when the day comes that he begins to acknowledge similar problems and similar background, his solutions tend to take the traditional AA names and shapes. He begins to speak of staying sober "a day at a time." He refers to his "Higher Power." He never fails to credit AA, in one way or another, for his sobriety. And frequently, he insists that he is only sure of his sobriety for "the next twenty-four hours."

By contrast, the person going into therapy in a confrontation group for alcoholics is allowed little leeway. Very soon after entering the group—be it hours or several meetings—he is confronted by his fellow group members about his alcoholism. He is only allowed to "play games" for a short while in any group before being called to task. His introduction to the group may not be much more painful and frightening than an alcoholic's first visit to an AA meeting, but soon after attending just a few meetings he will be called upon to talk about his feelings. He is rarely allowed to evade a direct confrontation.

There are innumerable experiences that one might describe for an alcoholic attending his first group therapy meeting. Groups vary according to tradition and method of the leader or therapist or of the sponsoring institution. They also vary according to the preferences of the group itself. In theory, the persons in any therapy group work as a unit, together with the therapist. The group's leader is not supposed to be a therapist but a "facilitator." One tradition that rarely varies in group therapy is that group leaders do not *openly* lead, answer questions, or set the pace.

A GROUP THERAPY EXPERIENCE

Your alcoholic attending his first group therapy session might simply be shown a chair, one of ten or twelve in a circle. He may then be left alone while the older and experienced people in the group deal with a particular member's problem. The problem being dealt with might be a particular member's recent altercation with his wife or boss or one of his children. (The group member's difficulties with this person in his life because of his drinking history have been explained previously.)

It might go like this:

Group Member Beatrice: "Well, Jim, are you going to share with us what happened this week when you told Beth you were *going to the store?*"

Jim: "I guess I could."

Beatrice: "You don't sound very willing, Jim. You don't have to, you know. You can tell us all to go fly a kite, if you feel that way."

Jim: "I know. It's just that, well, it seems so damn silly."

Beatrice: "There you go again, Jim! I think you just don't want to tell us about it. If you don't, why don't you just say so?"

Jim: "Hell, I don't mind telling you all. But who really cares? You all have been through it. You know what happened. Why not let somebody else talk about some really bad problem. Why let me take up everybody's time talking about something as trivial as that?"

Beatrice: "Jim, frankly I think you are being evasive. You're spending more time evading us than it would take to tell us about it. You just don't like to share your feelings with us, do you?"

Jim: "Damn it all, Beatrice, there you go making a mountain out of a molehill. You're never satisfied until you pick on me for a while, are you? Why don't you leave me along? Go tend to your own business for a change. You're not a therapist, you know. You haven't been around here much longer than I have!"

Group Leader: "Jim. You sound a little angry to me."

Jim: "Angry! I'm not angry! I'm just tired of some people worrying me about silly inconsequential details that shouldn't even concern them, that's all!"

Group Leader: "Jim, you may call it something else. It sounds like anger to me. Does anyone else hear anger?

Beatrice: "Do we? It's so obvious it's almost funny!"

Group Member Carlos: "Look at him! Jim's so angry now he's even forgotten what started it all . . . "

Another Group Member: "I guess I'm glad I'm not in Jim's shoes . . ."

This exchange of words and feelings is a common one for a group therapy session. But what has your alcoholic been doing while this was going on? Well, he has not been addressed yet and has not even joined in the exchanges. But he already begins to feel a little threatened. He knows that if they can test the emotions of one group member in that way, they can and will someday do the same to him. Notice that drinking has not been mentioned. It may not be for a whole hour at a time. But the group or group leader will eventually bring up the subject that is uppermost in the minds of the group.

The group therapy way of getting an alcoholic to admit his problem is to first get him accustomed to the idea of honestly looking at himself. In the foregoing exchanges Jim was obviously reluctant to discuss with the group the unpleasant experience he had had with his wife. It might have been that he had told her he was going to the corner grocery for a pack of cigarettes and that she behaved as if she thought he really wanted to get some beer. In the actual exchange between them, perhaps the words "beer" or "drinking" were never uttered. But both of them knew the source of the strain. By sharing this experience with his group, Jim might have been able to *ventilate* his feelings of anger and free himself of the constrictive frustrations that they were causing him. His anger was caused by his wife's obvious reluctance to accept his word (when he *really* had planned to buy cigarettes). But the experience was so threatening to him (and embarrassing) that he couldn't express his anger; he couldn't admit to that dirty word *anger* in front of the group. So, instead, he ended up getting angry with Beatrice because she persisted in asking questions.

At a feeling level Jim was getting the same vibrations or feelings from Beatrice over her questions that he had perhaps received from his wife in the original experience. By talking it all out and sharing all his feelings of anger with the group, Jim might eventually be able to share with the group his deeply felt yearnings for more freedom from suspicion from his wife. In this way he could eventually start talking about himself and his feelings in ways that would lead to changing his view of himself. He seems to see himself as a little boy suspected of deceiving his wife and of being treated as an inferior by her because of his alcoholism. He needs to see himself as a mature adult capable of discussing and accepting his wife's own fears and anxieties as natural and predictable. He will see that other members of the group have had and will share with him almost identical experiences. Several hours of this *feeling* experience on Jim's part with others in the group will help him to begin accepting himself.

By exposure and nearness to all these transactions, your alcoholic will begin to learn and experience and grow along with Jim and others, first vicariously and later directly.

In the view of many alcohologists, alcoholics all share a self-loathing that is best defined as depression. This hating of themselves could lead to serious consequences except for the use of defense mechanisms which all alcoholics employ to save themselves from really seeing how deep their depression or self-hate has gotten to be.

The goal of group therapy is to tear away—to remove— the defense mechanisms of denying, projecting, and rationalizing that the alcoholic has been building around his depression. To get a person to admit that he has been falsely denying the existence of an alcohol addiction problem to himself as well as to everyone else is difficult indeed. In group therapy it becomes easier than in other environments because others are going through the identical process right alongside him. The last good reason to not let his defenses down for the alcoholic is that he won't have anywhere to turn. He cannot admit that he is an alcohol addict (and therefore prohibited by all that makes sense from drinking alcohol) until he has somewhere else to turn, somebody to turn to, some haven to hide in.

A good group often provides this haven for the alcoholic who accepts the members of the group as his friends. Love is frequently spoken of in groups and frequently demonstrated. I shall never forget the first demonstration of this I ever saw.

I was an observer in a group at a large southern alcoholism treatment center in 1965. I had been attending the group with another observer all week. On the last day a woman came to the meeting late and interrupted the proceedings. She stood before the group, glowing, as she said:

"I'm going home this afternoon as all of you know. But I just had to come by and tell you how I feel about all of you. *I love you.* I believe I love each one of you as much as I have ever loved anyone before. You all have given me more to live for and taught me to love and appreciate life. I thank all of you from the bottom of my heart. Good-bye! I love you . . ."

You can be sure there wasn't a dry eye in the group. And I, myself, being a visitor to the group, felt almost ridiculous because I, too, had eyes filled with tears. But the feeling of gratitude and love that that woman expressed in such simple words could not be denied. It was really gut level, as we say in group therapy.

What that woman had learned in that group was what your alcoholic should be able to learn in a good group: to share his feelings with others, to learn to know people in the group as *feeling* persons (instead of as alcoholics, women, fat men, younger people, patients, or doctors), and that he will know them best of all! The idea is that everyone has feelings that are frequently hidden or suppressed within us so skillfully and deeply that no one gets to know us.

Some mental health experts believe that much mental

illness is caused (when it is not organic as some of it is) by the failure of a person to establish meaningful intimate relationships with at least one other person.

The meaning of such clichés as "no man is an island" and "everybody needs somebody" and "people who need people are the luckiest people in the world" repeats this same theme over and over. The ideal group therapy experience makes the group a living, loving unit in which all members learn to love and be loved by sharing their joys and sorrows, their hates and their fears, and their experiences in living. The more they share, the more they get from the group.

The minimum experience for an alcoholic in group is to learn to accept himself and to like himself despite his alcoholism. We hope he will also learn to feel loved and to love others despite his problem. When he can empathize with and accept other alcoholics as well as himself his maturity is even greater.

However, as in other psychotherapeutic experiences, it must never be forgotten that alcoholism is your alcoholic's basic and primary problem. If he does not accept the reality of his alcohol addiction—his inability to drink successfully and the severity of his problems caused by alcohol in the past—your alcoholic is not going to recover. It will matter little that he has learned to be loving and to feel wonderful about his fellow group members. As I have pointed out before, therapy groups for alcoholics can succeed only if the alcoholic is confronted with his problem and accepts it. Your alcoholic in group therapy is not going to experience recovery unless the group and the group leader understand his alcoholism. He may learn to love and be loved, to share and to accept from others many emotions and experiences wonderful to know and to experience. And it can help his recovery. But if his *alcoholism* problem and its *acceptance* isn't among the things learned, the group experience may do more *harm* than good. This is because the alcoholic has been misled into believing something false about himself, i.e., that there was a problem *more important* to him than his *alcoholism.*

The same evasion sometimes occurs in AA. The alcoholic seems to experience a spiritual awakening that has changed his life. If an accurate description of this experience does not include an open and free acknowledgment of the primacy of his alcoholism, it *must* be viewed with suspicion and concern.

Sometimes alcoholics report experiences with religion that are impressive and moving. But when the experience does not include a strong reference to his alcoholism as his basic problem, such spiritual experiences—with the rarest of exceptions—should be suspect.

I believe in the power of religion—yes, in the power of God—to change lives and to help alcoholics to recovery. But the number of times I have seen it operate successfully outside of a therapeutic alcoholism environment is almost zero. Several times I have been led to believe that a particular alcoholic has experienced a religious conversion and that he was no longer troubled by his addiction. But, so far—including the last one just a month ago at this writing—the alcoholic has returned to drinking. Sometimes it is precipitated with pills or by prescribed medication. But tranquilizers for alcoholics lead the alcoholic back to alcohol almost as surely as sipping wine or drinking a "little beer."

The true religious experience is perhaps the best way to cap the recovery of an alcoholic. But only after he has come to grips with his addiction. It is the finest "something else" to add to two full years of uninterrupted sobriety while in treatment. But it should be preceded with a focused attack on alcoholism itself. An illustration of this is the Twelve Steps of Alcoholics Anonymous. The first step is purely negative; it is focused sharply on alcoholism alone. "We admitted we were *powerless* over alcohol—that our lives had become unmanageable." This is the essential, the nitty-gritty step. Without it, the others cannot be expected to work and they will not. The key word is *powerless,* a concept our whole culture has taught us to deny. To help your alcoholic, the first step tells him his life has become *unmanageable.* Maybe if he can admit to that, he can correctly blame alcohol and understand his powerlessness over it. Once this step has been experienced—fully accepted—then the AA program wisely suggests that its new disciple come "to believe [as AAs do] that a power greater than ourselves" can restore "sanity." Beginning with the second step—but only after the purely negative admission of powerlessness over alcohol—all the other steps deal with your alcoholic's relationship to God or with moral principles.

Your alcoholic is going to recover when he experiences continuous constructive confrontation. Most experience in this country finds this should be about two years. Then, in my experience, there should be something added to your alcoholic's life. It may be a more understanding wife or a loved one or a more challenging career. It may be a new and meaningful relationship with people your alcoholic meets from day to day. It may be a new hobby or a new appreciation of the arts. Frequently it is a deep and lasting involvement with Alcoholics Anonymous. But this change is necessary to round out your alcoholic's new life. When that something extra is added to the three Cs, the prognosis is good.

Up to this point I have dealt only with group therapy and Alcoholics Anonymous without reference to the treatment facilities where group therapy is available.

Although Azalea Center in Nashville (which employs guided intervention with its clients) is an outpatient facility, we recommend when possible that treatment begin with admission to an inpatient facility. In 1975 the Joint Commission on Accreditation of Hospitals—which has been the standard-setter for American hospitals since 1919—began accrediting American alcoholism programs. (The Azalea Center program, as part of Samaritans, Inc., was among the first eighty-nine programs to be accredited.) I do not rule out the acceptability of nonaccredited facilities, but if no better reliable reference is available, I suggest that JCAH accreditation is a reliable guide.

Most good inpatient alcoholism programs combine the professional approach of encounter group therapy with AA. The two approaches blend well. Some centers emphasize one over the other. I favor those that emphasize *confrontation* in group over those emphasizing AA. I once heard the celebrated educator Dr. Robert M. Hutchins explain why he preferred teaching more "impractical" theory in law schools rather than the more practical. Unless the law student receives legal theory in school, Hutchins said, he would never again have to be troubled with it. Practical law experience would be plentiful when he left school. Likewise, I fear that unless *confrontation* is brought to bear on your alcoholic in the early part of his treatment, he may escape it forever. He might go to AA for years and never be confronted. It does happen. But if confrontation comes first, followed by the support of AA's Twelve Steps—and the fellowship and opportunity for a new life—then his chances are greatly enhanced.

I would avoid any alcoholism treatment facility that fails to recognize the value of AA. Trying to stay sober over the years without AA is like trying to get to heaven without identifying with a church. That's the hard way.

Don't confuse inpatient treatment with simple *detoxication.* There are many detoxication facilities for alcoholics across the nation but many of them do not have follow-up long-term treatments that must follow getting "dried out." Detoxication is important. It is often the first treatment process for many alcoholics who find it *physically* impossible to cut off the alcohol without endangering their lives or suffering the terrifying trauma of delirium tremens. But repeated detoxicating for your alcoholic—without the follow-up long-term treatment of AA or a professional facility—can develop into a harmful reinforcing process to *prolong* alcoholism rather than to *shorten* it. Most inpatient treatment centers have detoxication facilities on the premises or easy access to the service.

I advise you to use detoxicating for your alcoholic *only* on condition that he is going to follow up the physical cleansing process with the vastly more important psychological new birth process.

A third kind of treatment for alcoholics that is neither outpatient nor inpatient is the new day care treatment center. Here alcoholics come and spend the day in treatment and then go home at night. I believe this new method will gain favor across the nation as a practical and less costly system than inpatient centers and as a more intensive opportunity in a short period of time than outpatient programs. JCAH accreditation should be determined for these, too. It is available to them.

Most good inpatient treatment centers now favor an absolute minimum of five or six weeks of intensive treatment. Many that do not are planning to increase their minimum periods. More emphasis, too, is being placed on husband-wife relationships. Many inpatient facilities are *requiring* more than superficial social involvement by the nonalcoholic spouse. At our Samaritan Center, where we deal almost exclusively with indigent, homeless and familyless men and women, the minimum period of intensive treatment is sixty days. Samaritan Center believes so firmly in the influence of the concerned person that we will and do discharge a client whose concerned person will not participate in the program if that person has a viable relationship with our client. We have found that we cannot succeed if a concerned person is in the picture but won't come forward. Such is your importance to recovery as your alcoholic's concerned person!

11

The Problem of Feeling Level Understanding

The hardest attitude for alcoholics and concerned persons to acquire is a *feeling level* understanding of alcoholism. This problem confronts the counselor trying to help an alcoholic through his concerned person and confronts the concerned person for herself and her alcoholic. Its origins lie in the fact that hardly anyone really accepts alcoholism as a disease or even as something that happens to a person regardless of his morals or intelligence. Many polls show that an increasingly large percentage of the American population accepts alcoholism as a "disease." But my experience (with myself and many others) has convinced me that although a majority now say the words "alcoholism is a disease," most do not believe them at a feeling level. We can acknowledge the disease concept as long as it isn't brought home to us. Once it strikes in our own family or (horror of horrors!) when it strikes *me,* I have got to blame somebody or some *thing* and secretly—and above all—blame *myself.*

For an alcoholic, feeling level understanding means that he must deeply feel that for him and for every alcoholic, alcohol (or any mood-changing chemical) must be avoided as a poison as undesirable to swallow as lye, strychnine, or an overdose of morphine or heroin. Few alcoholics get this understanding and fewer concerned persons understand the need for it.

For everyone, alcoholics and nonalcoholics alike, feeling level understanding means to be able to feel empathy for an alcoholic whether he is drunk or sober. It means to feel that an alcoholic is a suffering human being without having any concurrent feeling of blame, rejection, superiority, or righteousness. Few of us achieve this.

Let's start with the problem of accepting alcoholism as a disease, as a nonculpable problem that can strike anyone who drinks a quantity of alcohol. Let's do this first on an intellectual level, not necessarily at "feeling level." Advocates of total abstinence for the entire population (government-enforced prohibition) should know by now that it won't work. While a smaller and smaller percent of the American population claim to be teetotalers, rarely anyone claims never to have tasted an alcoholic beverage. It is a fact that alcohol is as ever-present a substance in human affairs as milk, probably more available than milk. But a direct cause-and-effect relationship between large-scale consumption and alcoholism has not been demonstrated. Studies made from 1850 to 1962 and from 1930 to 1960 showed that France had the largest per person consumption of absolute alcohol among twenty nations studied and also the highest rate of alcoholism. But wait. Italy's alcohol consumption was second while its rate of alcoholism was ninth—about one-tenth that of France's!*

Alcoholism is often compared to diabetes. But those who

***Alcohol Education for Classroom and Community* by Raymond & McCarthy, editors, McGraw-Hill, New York, 1969.

hold alcoholics culpable say everyone is exposed to sugar and they don't eat it to get drunk. The fact remains that everyone who starts drinking doesn't do it to get drunk. Certainly not at the outset. It is known that some people are born alcoholics. The first time they try it, they like it so much they go on to get drunk. I have known several. My son, I suspect, was one. Marty Mann's *New Primer on Alcoholism* tells of an elderly woman in her sixties who was prescribed a bit of brandy each night instead of a sleeping pill. Within a short time this woman who had been a total abstainer all her life became addicted. She was soon requiring a bottle a night to sleep. Obviously, this woman did not intend to become addicted. Neither does *anyone.*

Unless we accept overweight or smoking as primarily moral issues, we should be able to accept alcoholism as a disease. If not, we might recall the story of the curing of the paralytic in the New Testament, told by all four apostles. When Jesus healed the paralytic by *forgiving* him his sins and was questioned by doubters, he changed his statement from *forgiving* to *healing.* Thus, we have high authority for not bothering to distinguish between what is an illness and what is a sin. A human problem by any name remains a problem to be solved.

Another reason people cannot readily accept the nonculpability of alcoholism when it strikes close to home is that it is too loathsome by any name to accept. They either deny that their own alcoholic's case is alcoholism or they find a myriad of reasons to justify the overt behavior and call it something besides what it is. This usually translates into the mistaken notion that by simply removing the reasons we will remove the problem. None of these attitudes works. Conduct your own poll. Ask ten people you know if they believe alcoholism is a disease. (You can do this mentally, if you like. You will probably know their answers without asking if they are old acquaintances.) If they answer yes, ask them if there are any social drinkers in their immediate family. Then ask if they believe one of these social drinkers could become an alcoholic. Almost all will tell you of their kin's "strong will power," or how carefully he drinks. No matter how often these friends repeat the idea that alcoholism is a disease, it is an abstraction, an unreal and unfelt conception. When brought home it is forgotten. The truth seems to be that almost all of us—because of the irresponsible behaviors manifested by a drunken person, perhaps—attach a moral stigma to alcoholism and to the alcoholic.

There is no such thing as simple will power. The connotations of such power are of a determination to do what one "wills" to do and not to do what one "wills" not to do. But behavioral psychology has made a strong case for showing that we all do what we are motivated to do. If a person is beautiful and popular, that person is not likely to gain excess weight. If she or he does, it will be quickly shed. The reason is the effect on other people. Friends and family will begin to show less appreciation for a beautiful person who has grown fat. We do what we are motivated to do by our environment and background. It is much easier for an alcoholic to remain abstinent while living or associating with other dry alcoholics than it is to do precisely the same thing while associating with heavy drinkers or frequenting bars. This should be remembered.

Apparently, the behavioral psychologists are right when they say that we are shaped (to what extent is the catch) by the rewards and punishments we receive. Generally speaking, we "will" to do what we are motivated to do. Remove the motivation and we may continue for a while but not for long unless we receive a reinforcement. Alcoholics who accept help and quit drinking are people who get the right motivation. That is what I am trying to help you provide in guided intervention. By the same logic it appears that persons who become alcoholics get that way, in part, because they have been more motivated toward behaviors that lead to alcoholism and *away* from behaviors that would prevent it.

You may say that your alcoholic was never "motivated" toward drinking, that his family and you have always opposed it, that you, yourself, have never drunk, or that alcohol has never been allowed in your home. So what? Neither has his family nor yours ever encouraged overeating for overweight people, or masturbating by your sons and daughters, or smoking. Yet all these behaviors are commonplace. They answer a *need* in the persons engaged in them. That need is the motivation. Overeating and smoking are both pleasurable and satisfying. Overeating seems to fill an emotional gap for some people. Smoking fills social as well as emotional needs for others. Masturbating offers emotional and physical relief. Remove the need (motivation) and the activity can be curtailed. Bear in mind, however, that alcohol is to overeating and smoking what morphine and heroin are to aspirin and coffee.

Thus far I have dealt only with an *intellectual understanding* of alcoholism. That is a problem that has to be overcome. But *feeling level* understanding is not only a deeper concept; for a recovering alcoholic and for you it is vital. Without it success will tend to elude you and your alcoholic.

Before trying to explain what I mean by feeling level understanding, I should acknowledge that whatever it is, apparently it is *relative* and it is *fleeting*. It requires constant reinforcing or we lose it and it varies in intensity from one person to another. That is why, as noted earlier, few alcoholics ever achieve it. Even when they do they can lose it with the passage of time by failing to reinforce it.

The intellectual understanding of alcoholism is neither fleeting nor relative. We either say and try to see alcoholism as a disease or nonculpable problem or we don't—in abstract terms. Whether we have that understanding *in our gut,* that is, at a feeling level, is a different matter.

A simple experiment that psychologists perform will help you understand the difference between *intellectual* understanding and *feeling* understanding. A person is fixed in a position in which he cannot move his head. He is asked to look at a lightbulb that blinks on and off. Each time it blinks, he is squirted in the eyes immediately following the light. This is done repeatedly for some ten or fifteen minutes. Soon, of course, the subject knows at an *intellectual* level that he is going to get squirted in the eye right after the light turns on. But, more important, he knows this at a *feeling* level.

The point is to prove that *feeling* level understanding is going to control the subject of the experiment, regardless of what he knows *intellectually*. To prove it, the subject is then told to watch while all apparatus used to squirt water is removed. Soon there is nothing present but the lightbulb. There is no possible way that person could be squirted again since there is no water anywhere near. When the subject confirms that he *knows*—or thinks he *knows*—there is no water anywhere near, he is instructed *not to blink his eyes* after the lightbulb turns on again. He soon demonstrates that he cannot hold his eyes open when the lightbulb flashes on. He will blink every time, no matter how hard he may try—intellectually—to tell himself that he is silly, crazy, and that he should be able to control his actions. There is no quick way to "tell" his *feeling self* that he need not blink.

This experiment's effects will wear off in a short time. It takes only fifteen minutes to condition a person to this and not very much longer for the conditioning to wear off. The point is that apparently no human being *can control* his actions if he has been properly conditioned to react in certain ways toward a certain stimulus. The subject knows in his conscious mind, intellectually, that there is no water to squirt him in the eye. But his unconscious self—his feeling self—knows better. His feeling self knows that when the lightbulb turns on, his eye is going to receive an unpleasant sensation. So he must close it to avoid it. The feeling self cannot understand an abstraction. It can understand only pain or a pleasant sensation.

This is the principle used for treating alcoholics in a few American treatment centers. It is called aversion therapy. Its shortcoming is that it will not last, it wears off, and it must be repeatedly reinforced. It is useful for some alcoholics who seem to remain immune to other kinds of communication and I think should be used more often. But it should always be used in conjunction with other therapy to keep the subject motivated to get reinforcement treatments. I suspect the reason it is not used more is that it works so well at first. The subjects and their families tend to think there has been a complete change. Then when the effect wears off for lack of reinforcements, everyone is thoroughly discouraged.

We used the aversion treatment with one hardened skid row alcoholic at Samaritan Center. Tim had been a chronic in jail, in workhouse, out again, drunk again alcoholic for seventeen years when he came to us. He was never able to stay sober longer than a week or two at a time. Then we tried the aversion treatment. Tim was hospitalized under a doctor's care. Once a day he was given emetine, a medicine that induces vomiting. Right after taking the emetine, he would get any alcoholic drink he requested. But having taken the emetine first, the drink would invariably be vomited very shortly after getting to the stomach. This procedure was repeated with Tim for five consecutive days. First emetine, then a drink, then vomiting. On the sixth day Tim was given the beverage without the emetine. You guessed it. He vomited the drink immediately. Tim knew *intellectually* that there was no emetine. But his stomach at this point could not get that abstract message. His stomach only understood one thing: When alcohol gets down here, throw it up!

When Tim came back to the Samaritan Center he had to get up from the breakfast table when they served apple juice! His *feeling self* associated the sight of apple juice with the wine that had made him sick even though he knew consciously —intellectually—that it was not wine. Tim also could not watch beer commercials on television the first few days after returning from the hospital. Eventually, of course, the effects of the treatment wore off. The physician who had helped us with Tim was unwilling to continue and Tim's head finally got the message to his stomach: When emetine is *not* present, the alcohol is going to make you feel *good* the way it always has! So Tim did get drunk again, although he had stayed sober for many months, the longest period in his adult life.

Later we were able to reach Tim's feeling level through the slow process of repeated drunken interruptions and readmissions to the center. Slowly, Tim got a more lasting kind of feeling level understanding that for him alcohol was poisonous, to be avoided at all costs. Tim's intellect was able to keep him sober about 97 percent of the time of his last few years, but his feeling level knowledge—that a little alcohol would make him feel good—was never extinguished completely. Tim would and did get drunk after many months of sobriety, irrespective of what seemed logical or natural. I think continuing the physical aversion treatments, by regular reinforcements, might have spelled the difference.

A true story I know makes the same point. A woman driver ran over a little dog, killing it. She felt upset enough to find out where the dog's owner lived. Then she knocked on the door and informed the owner of his pet's death. When she was through, the owner told her: "Don't worry about it anymore, lady! If I've told that dog once, I've told him a thousand times, *'Don't chase cars!'* "

Obviously, this dog owner did not know the difference between feeling level and intellectual level understanding. He thought he had done his duty by "telling" his dog with words not to chase cars. But there is a *feeling* way to "tell" a dog not to chase cars. Drive a car by the dog several times and when the dog chases the car, squirt a water gun at the dog with a previously prepared mixture of water and acid. Use just enough to cause pain but not permanent injury. A few of these treatments and dogs get the message: It is painful and unrewarding to chase automobiles.

What you are fighting with every alcoholic seems to be positive conditioning, as the psychologists call it. Your alcoholic's *feeling* self knows from repeated experiences that a little alcohol makes him feel good. He knows that if he is tired, uncomfortable, ashamed, has a headache, or is just bored—a few drinks will change him. It does not seem to matter that after that feeling good experience he is going to get nagged, feel sick, lose jobs, lose friends, or be ridiculed. The *feeling* self cannot see into the future at any time. The *feeling* self cannot grasp the idea of pain after the feeling good. The only way to change that is to make the alcohol cause the *pain* to the feeling self. But, the psychologists tell us, *positive* conditioning cannot be extinguished in most cases or at all. Because it is a *good* feeling—a positive experience—there is no way permanently to cause the feeling self to forget it!

I have noticed that whenever a group of alcoholics get together even for a serious purpose, there is one way to get smiles from all present. It is to start talking about drinking and drinking experiences. To recall drinking experiences among a group of chronic alcoholics who have stopped drinking and who are well on the way to permanent sobriety would seem to call for frowns and unpleasant expressions.

Yet it does not among most alcoholics. Even when they have been abstinent for long periods of time—five, ten, and fifteen years—recollections of drinking experiences bring nervous giggles and childlike responses of pleasure. I consider the alcoholic's response to talk of drinking—when he or she is unaware of being observed—a fair indication of how much *feeling* level understanding he or she may have of the illness.

The problem of acquiring this understanding is a mighty one. Aversion treatments are not available in many places and are not very helpful unless reinforcement by repeated treatments, continuing group therapy, or AA attendance can be assured. So the problem is to get this kind of deep understanding into the feeling system of your alcoholic.

Perhaps at this point you are beginning to despair of seeing your alcoholic succeed. You may have been putting him through the tests and situations I have described and found him wanting. If you have not, perhaps you should have because few alcoholics in the early stages of treatment acquire a feeling level *revulsion* of alcohol. That's the ideal. That's what we are looking for. The truth is that many alcoholics will live relatively peacefully and uneventfully the rest of their lives—never again drinking—and still not really have acquired the attitude that I have described.

Earlier in this book I used the word *internalize* with reference to the phenomenon I call feeling level understanding. *Webster's Seventh New Collegiate Dictionary* defines *internalize* as a verb meaning "to give a subjective character to: specif: to incorporate within the self as guiding principles." Giving something (such as the attitude toward alcohol) a *subjective* character, as Webster's defines internalizing, means "arising from conditions within the brain or sense organs and *not directly caused by external stimuli.*" In other words, when your alcoholic regards alcohol as something very bad and harmful to him—without having anyone present to influence him, no direct external stimulus—he has the desired attitude. He has "incorporated within [him] self as a guiding principle" the attitude that this chemical is a definite no-no.

I have been indicating ad nauseam that a physical revulsion for alcohol constitutes the acceptable feeling level attitude. I have a penchant for stressing ideas I feel strongly about. This point is frequently overlooked and therefore not pursued. I am convinced that if it were more often made the goal of alcoholism therapy a higher incidence of success would be the result.

The majority of alcoholism therapy-involved people I know divide into two groups. Those who frequently come from AA backgrounds tend to think that getting that revulsion for alcohol is impossible. They seem to believe that all alcoholics must go through life in constant fear of "taking that first drink" again. This attitude perhaps may be *nearer* the truth of the situation than the second one. This is one usually shared by professional people such as psychiatrists, psychologists, social workers, and others influenced by them. These people overemphasize the need for finding new ways of solving problems, for setting new goals, and for more self-understanding. These are necessary and helpful to recovery, and AA people know that too. But if the *ever-present addiction* is overlooked, then the alcoholic is susceptible to returning to his bottle. So the AA people recognize *positive conditioning* of the alcoholic (without calling it that) and recognize that it is practically never extinguishable. This causes them to continue a negative attitude as the *only* way for the rest of the alcoholic's life. The professionals sometimes fail to recognize the *positive conditioning* with alcohol (physical addiction). If so, they fail to fight it head-on and thus miss the mark with many patients.

Both attitudes are essential to lasting and permanent sobriety. You must at least make this physical revulsion—internalization of the knowledge that alcohol brings nothing but grief—an important part of your goal and the goal of your alcoholic.

Your alcoholic may never reach this point to your satisfaction or to his own. There is no "cure" for alcoholism. To be *cured* means to be a normal drinker with the ability to drink a moderate amount of alcohol without losing control. If there is ever going to be a cure, I am convinced it will be physical, a chemical change in the body. I don't doubt that science may someday produce this. I do not expect it in my lifetime and I caution you not to dream about it. It is a dangerous distraction from therapy.

What is your final goal? If you have followed my advice,

your goal is to keep your alcoholic in a treatment program for two years without interruption of sobriety. I also hope that during this period your alcoholic will find something new in life to take the place of his beloved booze. I suggest that this might be a new interest in you as a more desirable, understanding, and loving wife. It also might be a wonderful religious experience with lasting results or a deep involvement in the AA way of life. This seems to be the answer for more permanent cases of sobriety than anything else. (Almost all alcoholism treatments today either use or recommend AA affiliation and concepts.)

Above all, don't be discouraged if your alcoholic does not display a feeling level understanding of alcoholism as you and I want it. He may never reach that point. In the final analysis what counts is performance. If he stays sober for those two years, and goes to meetings of whatever kind, and shows other signs of starting a new life, get on your knees and thank God for your blessings. Never fight your alcoholic on the grounds that his *attitude* is not right. Try to accentuate the positive. You might keep that song in mind.

Here are more guidelines. If he is going to AA meetings (and no other form of therapy), then in the first few weeks and even longer he should go no less than five or six nights a week if at all possible. Most successful AA alcoholics I have known have done this. One saying one hears around AA clubhouses is to start by making "90 meetings in 90 days." That is excellent advice if there is no other therapy involved. That has been the salvation of most alcoholics I have known. After the early time is over, most alcoholics will naturally become more selective about meetings. They are not all of equal quality or attended by the same people. I would consider three or four meetings a week a good number for the first two years.

If your alcoholic receives no other help than AA (not even a good reestablished relationship to his church), then I would expect him to continue AA meetings well beyond the two years. As previously stated, almost all AA members who succeed continue going at least once a week. Above all, I caution you, don't ever encourage him to *stop* going to AA meetings if he wants to go.

If you live in a small community where there are not more than one or two meetings of the fellowship available, encourage your alcoholic to drive to nearby towns during the first few months of his program. Go with him, if possible. The ideal would be for you to attend at least one open meeting with him (where nonalcoholics are welcome) and to attend at least one or two Al-Anon meetings yourself.

If there is no AA group in your town, encourage your alcoholic to start one. It is easy to do and full directions and help can be obtained from your nearest AA group or by writing to Alcoholics Anonymous World Services, Box 459, Grand Central Station, New York, New York 10017. The same applies to Al-Anon. If there is not a group in your community, seek help from the nearest group or write to Al-Anon Family Groups, Inc., P.O. Box 182, Madison Square Station, New York, New York 10010.

If your alcoholic's program includes group therapy or other professional counseling, AA is still a helpful adjunct even if it is not stressed by your counselors. It is inconceivable to me that good alcoholism therapists would not encourage AA for him. If they oppose it, I would view them with concern. Conceivably, at some point, a therapist might have some negative views about AA. The therapist might feel that for a time your alcoholic was "using" AA as an "enabler." This might be his method of rejecting the professional person—and his alcoholism—on the phony grounds that "only" AA could help. Remember, there is no such truth. Use all the help you can get. Never accept total rejection of AA as good. It could be the worst mistake you could make in your alcoholic's program.

Sometimes an alcoholic may be slow about accepting help and even slower about going to AA. He may see AA as an almost public announcement to the world of his problem. Be patient with him. Let him "delay" going to AA if he does go to the other kind of alcoholism therapy. But never write off AA for good.

My view may be narrow. But I believe that any alcoholic who cannot at some point begin openly to speak of his alcoholism is one who still has not internalized his acceptance of alcoholism as a nonculpable phenomenon. It may take several years for your alcoholic to go to AA meetings or openly to talk about his alcoholism. But never give up the goal that that day will come. If your alcoholic acquires the desirable understanding of his alcoholism, he will accept himself as a worthy member of the human race who is also an alcoholic.

For you, the concerned person, to acquire a feeling level understanding of alcoholism as a nonculpable phenomenon, you must live with it for a long time. You must learn all you can about alcoholism, intellectually. You must associate with other concerned persons and share their experiences, their joys at their recovering alcoholics, as well as their frustrations, fears, anxieties, and angers. You must share their feelings by repeated exposure to them and by repeated attempts to share what they are going through. You must see and know of other successes and other failures. You must see and know other alcoholics, both likable and unlikable, pleasant and gentlemanly, unpleasant and boorish. You must learn to accept them, whatever their ways, words, and behavior toward you. When you begin to accept them as lovable and likable—in spite of their failings—and when you begin to understand what you have in common with *them*, as well as with their concerned persons, you will be getting a feeling level understanding of alcoholism. You will be able to give your alcoholic love and understanding, patience and firmness. You will help him to acquire an understanding and acceptance of himself as a worthy person and of himself as an *alcoholic* person.

12

What to Do about You

What about you, the concerned person of an alcoholic? You have problems and emotional needs apart from the problems and needs of your alcoholic person. You need strength to carry out your job as the psychological scalpel in this emotional surgery. But you are a person—a living, feeling being—not an inanimate instrument. You need to know *who you are* before you can resolve your problems and needs, just as a soldier must become acquainted with the components of a rifle before he can become a qualified marksman. In this chapter I will deal with some theories about your identity and how to get better acquainted with yourself.

I have recommended Al-Anon, alcoholism group therapy,

and a professional alcoholism counselor to guide you.* The least amount of help you should have is an AA or Al-Anon counselor suggested early in this manual. By all odds, if you have followed this advice, you have already begun to understand yourself better. In addition, every chapter of this book should have helped you to know yourself. Some are directed expressly to your problems with your alcoholic. Others attempt to explain your alcoholic to you. Chapter 9, although it is primarily aimed at explaining the alcoholic person, should have caused you to understand your own person. Now we (you and I) will deal only with you, your problems and needs. We will help you understand and accept yourself *as you are* not who you have been trying to convince yourself you are or who you have been afraid you are.

I believe one way to understand ourselves is to look at how much we disclose about ourselves to other people, to examine the people to whom we disclose some things and don't disclose other things and to ask ourselves *why*. In answering this *why*, I believe we will get new insights into ourselves that we have previously missed.

We have five easily understood levels of identity that we disclose to others. I call them level one, the Parlor self; level two, the Dining Room self; level three, the Kitchen self; level four, the Bedroom self; and level five, the Closet self.

THE PARLOR SELF

The most superficial self, the self you freely admit to being to anyone who asks, is your Parlor self. At Parlor depth you freely tell almost anyone that you are Mrs. John Brown, age forty-five, the former Jane Smith, college graduate, homemaker, mother, Baptist, and Democrat. Or, Mrs. Paul Gonzales, the former Hedda Stowkowski, Roman Catholic, or you are an Episcopalian, Republican, country club member. Your Parlor self also includes your address; the size, shape,

*I also recommend a beautiful little paperback entitled *Why Am I Afraid to Tell You Who I Am?* by John Powell, S.J., Argus Communications of Niles, Illinois 60648

and color of your house; furnishings; cars; landscaping. It also includes the visible facts about yourself, whether blonde, brunette, slender, heavy, tall, short, light or dark complexioned. These are statistical facts you disclose to a questioner on request.

This Parlor self is the conscious thinking-in-words, communicating-in-words you. This is the you anyone can meet at a social gathering and learn about without trying hard. You don't bother to tell much more because you assume they do not want more. You base this assumption on a feeling habit acquired over the years in meeting many strangers under similar circumstances. Then if you meet someone at a casual gathering and that person begins to ask too many questions of you—even questions not of an intimate kind—the chances are you become offended and try to get away from that person. You may get to know this person later and ask yourself why in the world you did not respond openly to his inoffensive inquiring. You may be able to admit later that his questions were not improper, or could not really be judged as anything but friendly. Yet, you continue to reject many questions from other strangers who ask the same kind of questions, just more than the usual new person. You continue to be dissatisfied with yourself over this feeling habit especially when repeated experience tells you that you may not be getting to know as many desirable, new, and interesting people as you would like.

Understanding the reasons for this discomfort that you cannot change is a part of the process of getting to know who you are. But we are only at the preliminary stage. Let's consider the second depth, the Dining Room self.

THE DINING ROOM SELF

This second level of your *self* is merely more detailed than your Parlor self. At Dining Room level you get into your middle name, your parents', children's, husband or wife's names, ages, birthdays, minor personal characteristics, and details about your own everyday likes and dislikes, favorite colors, people, television programs, movie actors, political candidates, brands of clothing, food, and cars. This level of your identity opens up other problems as your Parlor self did. These problems come because of your lack of flexibility.

You change in some areas. You change some of your likes and dislikes but are reluctant to explain these changes at Dining Room level. You become disenchanted with a particular brand or a person or a group. But because you have over the years adopted an attitude of consistency at all costs, you are afraid of change and you begin to live little white lies. You continue associating with friends of whom you disapprove, you continue buying from firms you dislike, and you doggedly continue to pay membership fees in a club or society you no longer like.

Your Dining Room level self is more troublesome than the Parlor self because it is deeper and a little closer to the real you than the bare statistics of your *level one* self. You may have selected your marriage partner at Dining Room level. (Although many people may share a bedroom with their intended marriage partner before the nuptials, only Dining Room level information about themselves is likely to be disclosed. To share a bedroom is not necessarily to reach your Bedroom level self.) It is also at Dining Room level that you may be divorced, choose a job, a neighborhood, school, clothes, automobile, a hobby, most of your friends, and sometimes even your religion.

If you make such crucial decisions in your life as whom to marry and what religion to profess in your Dining Room level of identity—exploring the same superficial information about others—you are likely to have serious emotional problems. One way to restore order in your life is to examine your functioning levels when making decisions. Selecting an automobile may be all right at level two, the Dining Room self, but selecting friends calls for a deeper level and selecting a lifelong mate for marriage needs the deepest level of all.

THE KITCHEN SELF

Level three, the Kitchen self, is appropriate for choosing friends. It is that level of your self that you share with your husband, children, parents, and closest friends. Depending on how broad your previous level is, your Kitchen level may include your fears of heights, dark, enclosed places, airplanes, and other minor things. It may include the fact that you color your hair, that you are self-conscious of your weight or foot size, or that you don't like people of a different color or speech accent. It may include the fact that you have tried to stop smoking and can't, that you know you eat too much but continue to do so, that you spend more than you should and cannot save money, or that your parents have less than a high school education. Or it may be that they are unsophisticated country folk or belong to a group foreign to your social circle. Your Kitchen level disclosures don't present you with problems you cannot handle if you have a fairly wide group of people with whom to share these facts. It should help to clear up problems of your Dining Room level (if you have had them) by being more open and truthful at Kitchen level than you were able to be at that level. This will compensate for the problems of being less than frank and open and living with some little white lies at Dining Room level.

Your Kitchen level identity should be a comfortable and happy one. Your Parlor and Dining Room levels should be, too, but you are more likely to survive strains and problems in those levels if your Kitchen self is a happy one. You should be able to relax and enjoy family and friends in your Kitchen self, shoes off, washing dishes, having a cup of warmed-over coffee, or eating leftovers. Your Kitchen identity is informal, nonpretentious, and truthful.

YOUR BEDROOM AND CLOSET LEVELS

Next is your Bedroom self. This is the level you share largely with marriage partners in matters of sex, with parents and very close friends in matters of marital problems, and with doctors or lawyers in matters related to their fields. In my mind, your Bedroom self is merely a deeper extension of your Kitchen self. You may be the kind of person who doesn't draw a distinguishable line between your Kitchen and Bedroom identities. Some of your intimate friends may share as much of your Bedroom self as your husband, parents, and children. If so, you may not have a very discernible Bedroom level. More about this later.

After these levels of your identity comes the most troublesome, the Closet level self. To this level of your self you assign all those facts about which you feel shame, fear, or embarrassment. You refuse to share any of these feelings about yourself with anyone. You know, you tell yourself, that no one will understand them. No one will respect you after knowing that your first child was born seven months after your wedding. No one will accept you if they know your father was an alcoholic or only moderately successful in life. No one will find you attractive if they know how small your breasts really are. No one will respect your morals if they know that you once had an affair or that you once had an abortion. Many are the things you may try to bury in your mind, things you try never to think about, things you never knowingly share with anyone.

You may not have a Bedroom identity. Your Bedroom identity may in fact be your Closet self, the self you refuse to share with anyone. In your sexual relationship with your husband you may never have told him that you never experience a climax. You may never tell him that you desire him more often than he seems to know. You may not tell him you desire him at all if you still belong to that segment of our culture that considers such a disclosure by a woman as unseemly.

You also may never share with anyone else the fact that your husband has beaten you physically as well as emotionally. If you have been living without ever sharing your Closet self with someone, you are likely to be a person with emotional problems, problems approaching in severity your husband's drinking problem.

It is my conviction that there should be only the smallest Closet level self for emotional health. I believe you will find life more tolerable—even happier—by sharing your secrets with at least *one* other person. Anyone who has had the slightest experience in counseling—whether minister, priest, psychiatrist, or other—has learned that ventilating, disclosing worrisome secrets, is a common human need. Keeping things bottled up in you can be as bad for your mental health as constipation is to your physical health. Regardless of how hard you may find it, "letting it all hang out" can be one of the most cleansing and rewarding experiences of your life. The chances are that your deep, dark secrets are no more unique or shocking than the experiences of the person to whom you disclose them.

Beyond even your Closet level identity is the unconscious or subconscious self, the self you have no easy way of knowing and may not even need to know, the self partially revealed in your dreams or that can be brought out in hypnosis or by years of psychoanalysis. This last identity I will not attempt to deal with here. I have not found it necessary in alcoholism counseling to get any farther than the Bedroom and Closet levels. When deeper psychotherapy seems advisable, I recommend psychiatrists.

The need—or even the inescapability—of having distinct Parlor, Dining Room, Kitchen, and Bedroom identities is a natural phenomenon. We literally cannot share with everyone all the intimate details of our life simply because there is no way to communicate that much information. To say the least, not everyone would be interested. The same can be said of each deepening level of identity. We are not likely to share as much at Dining Room level as at Kitchen level because our Dining Room level friends are less interested in our private lives than the people at Kitchen level. You can repeat this principle down through Bedroom and Closet levels. But when you reach Closet level I believe you need to share with at least one person (if not more) for your own good. In selecting this person I suggest that you trust your *feelings.* If you don't feel comfortable with a person, do not ask that person. If you don't have someone to use, go to a professional. Go to your pastor, physician, lawyer, or a professional alcoholism or marriage counselor. But by all means go to someone. Remember, the more free you grow to feel about yourself—from Parlor to Bedroom—the more satisfied you obviously are about *who you are.*

If you have a big Closet level self that you are afraid to talk about, the reason is obvious. You do not like this level of yourself. This disapproval of yourself can bring you problems because you can never bury secrets effectively. They will resurrect at the most inappropriate times or cause you such physical problems as stomach ulcers and digestive problems. They will cause you to compensate in harmful ways and in the end the compensations will be more damaging to you than disclosing your secrets would ever be.

If you think you have a valid reason for not sharing your secrets with someone else, consider the facts. The truth is that your secrets are a part of you, a part of your identity, and in hiding them you are ashamed of yourself. But once you unload your secrets you make the burden lighter. The secret is no longer a secret. It can no longer frighten you as much because in sharing it you discover the world doesn't stop, the sun still sets, and the person with whom you share it still regards you as the same person as he saw in you before hearing your terrible tale. You are by appearance—and therefore, in fact, in that area—the same person as before. And you are not the same person (in another area) as the person to whom the terrible secret happened. Your secret is now something *in the past tense.* That makes it null and void in the present. It is yesterday's truth, yesterday's reality. But only today's memory. It is done. It is not happening now. You can never change the fact that it happened. It is a part of your experience. But you need to accept it only as part of your experience—a little bit of who you are—the same way you accept other accomplished facts—your aging process and other inevitable phenomena. But they need not dominate your life.

Your goal should be to *love* your identity. It is you. How can you love anyone else's identity if you can't love your own. So, you are an ex-convict, or so, you once had an abortion. You cannot change those facts but you are not a *convict* today, and you are not *aborting* now. Who knows that anyone else might have done under the circumstances and background at the time these things happened to you? Only God knows and we are advised not to judge others, so how can we intelligently judge ourselves?

The American playwright Eugene O'Neill believed everybody wears masks in life. The characters in some O'Neill plays wear masks that they remove only for special people.

Shakespeare said that all our world is a stage and we are merely players, pretending to be somebody we are not. When we wear masks as O'Neill's characters do onstage, it may be a sign of serious emotional problems. We are frightened and uncomfortable with our real or imagined selves. It may be necessary to wear masks sometimes but only when we know what we are doing and for a specific purpose. Sometimes generals, ministers, lawyers, and teachers seem to play roles. But the mature person is himself regardless of his profession. If he seems to be wearing a mask or playing a role, he knows it and it has become a part of him. The *mask is him* in fact for the while he wears it. *He is his role.* If generals leave off their uniforms and ministers their robes and appropriate mannerisms, they don't impress us. They are less effective.

You too must play a role, *your role,* and become that person. You must be a parent and scold and get upset at certain times to hold your place in the lives of your children and to shape their future. You must speak and act in certain ways, sometimes, even if you don't really feel it. But you must know you are acting and for a purpose. And you must acknowledge it in some way, to some person. This is sometimes as real as your other identities. But you should know what you are doing and what your feelings are. If you don't, you are living in a false world. You may also be a neurotic or a fraud in relation to yourself. The more you can narrow down the person you are supposed to be and are expected to be with the person you want to be—without straining truth—the happier you will be.

Your most important identity is the *feeling* you. You may now know this self. But look around and learn. There is truly a new generation of Americans in the sixties and seventies who wear long hair, blue jeans, beards, and who advocate what an earlier generation called trial marriage. They are this way because of their reaction against our mask-wearing habits and traditions. Their informal—sometimes not even clean—dress and way of living is a *backlash* against our almost total rejection of our *true* selves. These young people know this and make no bones about how they feel about it and about us. I think they frequently go too far in judging everything at a feeling level. But consider the words of Carl R. Rogers, one of the most influential psychologists of our time. Rogers says that "when an activity *feels* as though it is valuable or worth doing, it *is* worth doing. Put another way, I have learned that my total organismic sensing of a situation is more trustworthy than my intellect" (Rogers's italics).*

I cite Rogers to make a point. The life-style of the new generation is not accidental. It was planned. It seems clearly to be the fruition of Rogerian nondirective psychotherapy, now a philosophy. It may not suit you and me as a guide for how to live, but it can be of inestimable value to you in understanding yourself and your problems. We who were born before, during, and after the Great Depression of the thirties and who came of adult age during and following World War II are as far removed in many ways from the "feeling" philosophy of Rogers as we can be. We were of the "men don't cry," "ladies never whistle," "children should be seen and not heard" generations and we were taught to "eat everything on your plate" at every meal. We were taught always to hide and suppress our true feelings. Our alcoholic loved ones were taught the same. That *contributed* to their looking for escape in the bottle.

Psychologists and psychiatrists say that not having at least one intimate person with whom to share our emotional burdens is a leading cause of mental illness. It is true that we cannot express and disclose our feelings everywhere. If we do, we are not going to be invited to many places. At Parlor level none of us likes to break down and shed tears. Not even at Dining Room level. But we need to be able to cry at Kitchen level, sometimes, and if not there, by all means at Bedroom level. If not with sobs and tears, then at least with open and unguarded crying kinds of words.

You must learn to drop the mask, leave off the role-playing of wife, mother, polite member of the church choir, or Girl Scout leader long enough to discover the real you, the feeling person behind all the masks, body stances, and facial expressions. Your alcoholic drops his mask when he gets drunk and feels relief even though it is short-lived. But you

**On Becoming a Person* by Carl R. Rogers, Houghton Mifflin Co., Boston.

may not know how to drop yours and be your basic feeling self.

Where can you learn to drop your mask and get to know yourself as you truly are?

Where can you find people who will really care about your feelings and even help you to know—to identify—your true feelings?

Where can you find people who will tell you how they honestly feel about you and help you to see yourself as others see you?

Where can you get all these things without a lot of mumbo jumbo or psychiatry and still not get hurt?

The answer to these four questions is the same two words: *group therapy.* Get into a professional group and all these things can happen.

You will drop your mask, slowly or rapidly, as you like, but you will be able to because you will see and feel—you will *experience*—the pleasure of being *just you* with other people.

You will—in time—get to know that these people care about your feelings and you will learn to "hear" and care very much about their feelings.

They will tell you honestly how they feel about you and you will acquire that great gift of which the poet Robert Burns wrote, "to see yourself as others see you."

With this kind of help you will be strong and happy. You will be able to help your alcoholic as you never can in any other way.

This book by itself is not likely to make any great change in your manner of living. But with group therapy and AA or Al-Anon, a change will be almost inevitable. Your first goal then will be to learn about the feeling you. That is where many of your problems lie. Who is that?

The feeling you is the person who grieves and cries internally or behind closed doors about your alcoholic's insults, threats, violence, and his tragedy.

The feeling you is the person who has for years and years lived in dread of the day your children would discover that Daddy was an alcoholic and be traumatized forever. But the feeling you suppressed and hid those fears and never admitted them to anyone. The feeling you lied and covered up and became sick or worked long hours and strained body and mind to protect everyone from the terrifying truth.

The feeling you is the person who began seeing more and more evidence of this tragedy in action and spent many months hiding it from yourself.

The feeling you is the mother who continued to refuse to talk about the situation even when the children started seeing it.

The feeling you is the person who has been reading this book and saying to yourself that it makes sense but you are still unable somehow to take the first step.

The feeling you is the person who is afraid of disappointment, afraid of another setback, afraid of the risks involved.

The feeling you is a person living in dread of being beaten, threatened, or perhaps left penniless and husbandless if you try guided intervention.

The feeling you may be a foolish-hearted woman who keeps reliving the past, thinking "He'll wake up and see the light if I am just patient enough." And, knowing in your heart that this is not ever going to happen.

The feeling you may be honestly more satisfied to suffer the familiar hurts and damage of your alcoholic than to venture to be hurt by new and unknown people. Again I quote the psychologist Rogers. He insists he has found that "the facts are friendly." Or, as the much older biblical wisdom has it, "The truth will make you free."

Here once more are some of these truths about you:

You cannot change your past. If you have suffered, sinned, made terrible mistakes, reared children who seem to stand for or contradict everything you feel is basic and important, you still cannot change what *has been.*

Yesterday is gone forever. Tomorrow has not arrived. What counts most for your emotional health and survival today is what is true, alive, and before you, *today.*

You need to start acting now. Today. You cannot "will" any kind of change for what you did yesterday, what your spouse did yesterday, and what your children or anyone else did yesterday. That is done. Who you are in great part is not who you were yesterday (which helped to shape you), but who you are today.

Today you are the person reading this book, leafing these pages, taking a hard look at yourself now as it comes to an end. You are the person who has been reading this catalog of hope. You are the person who needed this. You are a person who has known suffering and who will know much more suffering if you continue the way you were yesterday and the day before that and the one before that and last month and last year. They *have been.* They are no longer reality today. Whatever marks they have left on you are there but they are only marks, only scars.

The hurts of yesterday are not what is hurting you today *unless you let them hurt you.*

Those pains are not present today *unless you are purposely keeping them alive.*

The mistakes you made yesterday, last month, and last year are not mistakes that you are living with today. You recognized them so you know they are mistakes. Thus, you put them out of your life.

Today, all you have are the echoes, the fuzzy memories of these mistakes. Some you exaggerate in your mind. Some you minimize in your mind. They are no bigger and no smaller than you make them today. They are yours to handle today *the way you want to handle them.*

A NOTE TO PROFESSIONALS

Helping Your Alcoholic Before *He or She Hits Bottom* is a new approach to alcoholism treatment that places the *initial* responsibility for getting treatment on the nonalcoholic concerned person rather than on the alcoholic. The hypothesis is that the majority of all alcoholics who accept treatment do so as a result of outside pressure. Guided Intervention, the method of the book, structures the pressure. Several agencies have been moving in this direction in the last several years. A 1966 pamphlet entitled "How to Help An Alcoholic Who

Insists He Doesn't Need Any Help"* recommended family education and described a family confrontation technique. The Johnson Institute of Minneapolis favors family guidance and family confrontation.**

Industrial alcoholism programs in the United States have been enjoying a high rate of success simply by getting employers to insist on treatment for alcoholics as a *condition* for continuing employment. The need for Guided Intervention was implied by the Rev. Joseph L. Kellermann when he cited these programs as a model that might be applied by families as well as employers.†

Guided Intervention is a step-by-step approach to lead an alcoholic into treatment. It begins with gentle, indirect psychological suggestion rather than with the trauma of family confrontation.

Helping Your Alcoholic Before *He or She Hits Bottom* calls for the "absolutely selfless love" described by Rea Killoy Stoll in "Therapy With A Two-By-Four: A Challenge to the Therapist".†† It holds that the greatest love is a willingness to risk the termination of a relationship rather than continuing the risk of a virtual suicide pact. It often succeeds without direct pressures on the alcoholic just as industrial alcoholism programs can succeed without firing.

*R. Michael Swift, Executive Director, Fairfield County (Connecticut) Council on Alcoholism, 1966.

**The Johnson Institute, 7325 Wayzata Boulevard, Minneapolis, Minnesota 55246.

†Rev. Joseph L. Kellermann, Paternoster delivered at 1975 Annual Meeting of the Alcohol and Drug Problems Association of North America.

††Rea Killoy Stoll, *University of Kansas Journal of Social Work,* 1973.

Index